Bargello is easy, fun & creative!

Using only one simple stitch and unbounded only by your imagination, Bargello has fascinated stitchers for centuries. Its look can be as contempary as the latest street fashions or a classic as a Renaissance chair -- all with the same stitch and patterns.

Bargello Revisited is the most comprehensive book on this delightful form of needlepoint in print. You'll learn
> ~ How to stitch Bargello
> ~ The types of thread to use
> ~ How to adapt any pattern to your choice of colors
> ~ How to solve common problems in Bargello

Complete with over 30 projects for stitchers at all levels and including 13 templates to create outlines for Bargello, you can mix and match to make your projects unique.

A springboard to creativity, this book will help you develop color schemes, choose Bargello patterns and finish your needlepoint with flair. Everything from a simple Bargello ornament to an elegant tool tote and evening bag is included.

So take up your needle, get some canvas, and get inspired!

I Bargello, do you?

Keep Stitching
Jant

Bargello Revisited
Janet Perry

To my Mom, Petey, who has always been my biggest fan
and
to Steve, who is absolutely the best

Credits & Acknowledgments

You can't write a book in a vacuum and this one is no exception, so I want to thank a bunch of people.

Those stitchers who keep the wonderful tradition of Bargello alive.

Toni Randall, my dear friend, who gave permission to use her templates and who has been so supportive of all my work.

Holly McGuinness, who proofread parts of the book and who was unfailingly generous with her ideas to make this book better.

Barbara Snook, the late British author, who inspired me more than I can say with her wonderful Bargello books.

Maggie, Thomas, & Anna, my kids, who have honed their artistic sensibilities by deciding what colors to use; I couldn't do it without you. You may not do needlepoint, but you know what makes a good design

My DH, Steve, who rarely complains about needlepoint taking over much of the house and much of my life.

brown paper packages, Conjoined Creations, Kreinik, Needlepoint. Inc., Rainbow Gallery, River Silks, Gloriana Threads & Ty-Di Threads, who generously supplied threads for these projects.

My wonderful modelstitchers, Sharon Brownstein, Sondra Dyer, Diane Malas, Holly McGuinness, Pat Miller, Linda Nelson, Nancy Robertson, Pat Peter, Phyllis Bush, Cheryl Jarosh, Marietta Douglas, and Alice Tryon - your help made what seemed impossible, possible.

Susan Thompson; who supplied finishing services, you're a champ.

Cheryl Jarosh and K. Lyn Dallman; who proofread so wonderfully.

The folks at Axess Printing who provided printing and publishing services and for helping to make my dream a reality, and whose patience and professionalism is amazing.

Wakko, Dot, and Astro, my three cats, who keep watch while I work.

Table of Contents

Projects

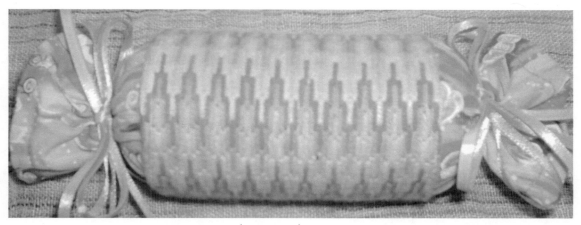

Spires Needleroll (page 56)

Hand-dyed Mini-sock (page 37)

Twisting Ribbons Mini-sock (page 41)

Assymetrical Zig-zag Mini-sock (page 46)   Topsy-Turvy Pillow (page 48)

Counterchange Mini-sock (page 50)   Four-way Bargello Pincushion (page 52)

Rainbow Hot Air Balloon (page 65)

Bargello Tool Tote (page 35)

Lines Mini-sock (page 58)

3-D Christmas Tree (page 60)

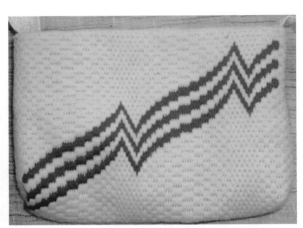

Hungarianpoint Mini-sock (page 67)   Op Art Purse (page 62)

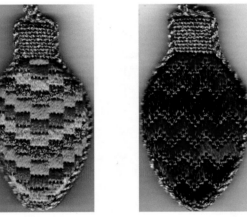

Christmas Lights
(page 43)

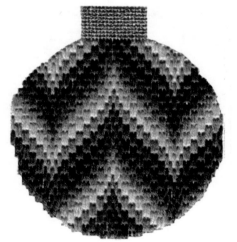

Bargello Mitten (page 72) Scissors Case (page 69)   Quick & Easy Round Ornament
(page 64)

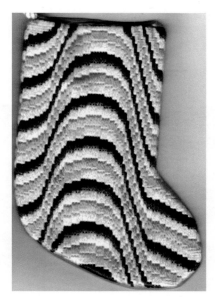

Free Curve Mini-sock (page 74)

Carnation Bellpull (page 76)

Tahiti Mini-sock (page 78)

Sweetheart Mini-sock (page 81)

Bargello Cell Phone Case (page 39) Hungarianpoint Line Checkbook Cover (page 97)

Pink of Perfection Heart (page 79) Scrolls Bargello Tote (page 87)

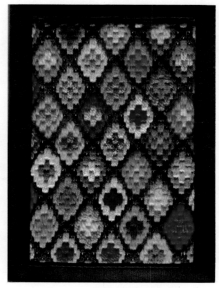

Dots Coin Purse (page 83)

Swoosh Mini-sock (page 85)

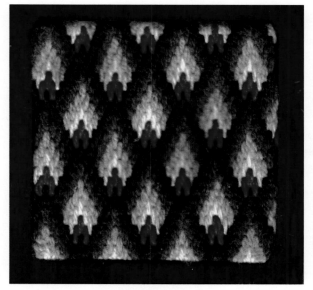

Flames Coasters (page 89)

Santa's Mini Sock (page 91)

Odd Number Mini-sock (page 93)

Moonlight & Gold Jewel Box (page 95)

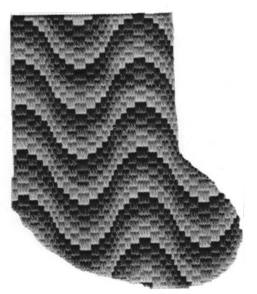

Big Curve Mini-sock (page 54)

The Basics
What Is Bargello?

That wonderful old wing chair covered in needlepoint. Your college French teacher's gorgeous pink dining room chair seats. A lovely evening bag. You've probably seen and loved Bargello patterns, and perhaps you are familiar with them already. I fell in love with Bargello the first time I saw it (in about 1971) and have loved it ever since. It is one of the easiest forms of needlepoint to stitch, and it gives amazingly different results depending on the colors and threads used. You can use many kinds of threads, there is an unlimited selection of designs, and best of all, it's fast and easy to stitch.

Bargello has been popular for over 500 years, but its origins are a mystery. There are a few Medieval pieces which have patterns which look like simple Bargello. The technique probably evolved from the simple zig-zag patterns you can see in couching, folk embroidery. and Medieval church needlework.

In the 17th and 18th Centuries, this type of needlework took a giant step and became what we recognize today as Bargello. In fact, two of the common names for this form of needlework come from the needlework of this period. Several chairs in the Bargello Palace (now a museum) are covered in a recognizable Bargello pattern. The Palace is in Florence, hence the second common name, Florentine Work.

Another legend about the origins of the needlework gives rise to yet another name, Hungarian Stitch. The legend goes that a Hungarian princess married a Florentine prince and brought this form of needlework with her. This story is largely discounted, although the term Hungarian work is still used to describe Bargello which has steps of two different lengths.

Flame Stitch is another name sometimes heard for Bargello. It reflects the flame-like look of many Bargello line patterns.

Stitching Bargello

If you know how to make a Satin or Gobelin Stitch, you know how to do Bargello. Bargello patterns are made up of groups of Satin Stitch, one or more per level, which move up or down in a regular pattern, called the step. These levels and steps form a pattern which is called a line. Many Bargello patterns move across the pattern in a zig-zag or curved line, these are called line patterns. Others form open or closed shapes, sometimes called fill patterns. In this book's patterns, you will find examples of all types.

To stitch Bargello, bring your needle out of the canvas. Then go up (or down) the given number of threads, usually four, and bring the needle back into the canvas. The diagram on the next page shows one stitch.

FIGURE 1: SINGLE BARGELLO STITCH

The length of the stitch can vary, but it generally goes over an even number of threads.

The next step may be right next to the first stitch, forming a step of more than one stitch, or it may be up or down a step.

 If the stitch is on the same step, repeat the process until all the stitches on the step are complete.

 If the stitch is on another step, go up (or down) the listed number of threads, and make the second stitch. The diagram below shows one step.

FIGURE 2: ONE BARGELLO STEP

Continue in this way until the pattern line is complete.

When your pattern is moving UP, stitch from the top of the stitch to the bottom, when the pattern is moving DOWN, stitch in the opposite direction. This creates the thickest coverage on the back of the canvas. The stitches lay better and will wear longer. Figures 3 and 4 show the right (3) and wrong (4) look on the canvas back.

 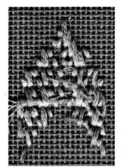

FIGURE 3: RIGHT WAY FIGURE 4: WRONG WAY

This book is organized into three main sections. This section, the first, has background information, instructions on how to stitch Bargello, and a section on problems which often occur and ways to solve them. It finishes with sections of color schemes and adapting patterns to your taste.

The next section contains templates for outlines to be filled with Bargello patterns. While many of the projects use specific templates, you can use pretty much any template with any pattern. So go hog wild, use up your stash of threads, and make a whole Christmas tree of ornaments in Bargello.

The final section has the projects. Each one has a materials list, step-by-step instructions, and a chart of the pattern (or patterns). There is a bibliography of great Bargello books, mostly out-of-print but easy to find. And a listing of manufacturers of the supplies used, and a list of other places to find wonderful of fantastic Bargello projects available for sale.

Problems and how to Avoid Them
"Needlepoint Dandruff"

This is a delightfully descriptive name for those flecks of white canvas which show through no matter how thick the thread is. Their presence makes even the most beautifully stitched piece look amateurish. They happen most often with straight stitches like Bargello.

Needlepoint Dandruff occurs when darker threads are covering lighter colored canvas. It is especially noticeable when the canvas is white.

The easiest method to control this is to use colored canvas. In fact, this method is so common that a type of ecru 13 mesh canvas is called Bargello canvas. The dark tan color makes the dandruff less apparent. In addition to ecru canvas, you can use a canvas in a pale shade of the predominant color of the threads. I also like to use pewter or eggshell canvas, as these blend with most colors.

But using colored canvas might not completely solve the problem. So a better solution is to color the canvas before you begin to stitch. This can be done with paint, or fabric marking pens (dye-based, like FabricMate). Color the entire canvas. It doesn't have to be an even layer of color, but all threads should be colored. Chose a color which is in the dominant color family and close to the lightest shade. The dandruff will not appear because your eye is tricked into thinking that the specks are the same color as the stitching.

I used this method for a navy blue Bargello background and there is not one speck of dandruff!

Threads Coming Undone

Threads come undone because Bargello stitches are longer and looser than many other needlepoint stitches.

There are three ways to solve this problem. The first is to use a "waste knot" to begin your threads and to park the thread off to the side when you are finished with it. The second way is to use the Bargello Tuck. The final way to start and end threads is the L Stitch, adapted from Japanese embroidery.

Waste Knot Method: A waste knot is made on the front of the canvas, a few inches away, in a straight line, from where you will be stitching. As you stitch, be sure to pierce the tail of the thread. When you get to the knot, pull on the end and cut just underneath the knot.

To end a thread pull the tail out of the front of the canvas in a straight line from where you stopped stitching. As you stitch, be sure to pierce the tail of the thread When you get near the tail cut if off.

It is important to pierce the tail of the thread as you stitch, otherwise it might work itself out.

Bargello Tuck: This is a method Jean Hilton recommends for starting many stitches. It adds an additional layer of security which is fantastic for Bargello and works well for many other stitches as well. You use the same method for starting and ending the thread.

This cannot be done on the first thread of a piece as it requires some stitching on the back to work.

Begin by running your thread through about 1" of stitches on the back. Pull the thread through until the tail disappears.

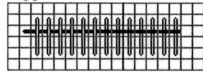

FIGURE 5: BARGELLO TUCK - STEP 1

Now go back, and in the opposite direction, pull the needle through about 1/2" of stitches on the back.

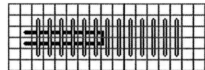

FIGURE 6: BARGELLO TUCK - STEP 2

L Stitch: This method is adopted from Japanese embroidery and was taught to me by Shay Pendray. It consists of two very tiny stitches on the front of the canvas. Begin by bringing your needle out the canvas to the front. Bring the needle back down into the canvas in the hole immediately above the original hole. This forms one leg of the L.

Bring the needle back out of the canvas in the original hole. This time, bring the needle back into the canvas in the hole to the right of the original hole. This forms the other leg of the L.

FIGURE 7: L STITCH

The L will be covered by later stitching.

You can end the thread the same way, either in a open area of canvas or by using your needle to bury the tiny stitches under an existing stitch.

Threads Pulling Away from Each Other

When you stitch Bargello, sometimes blocks of stitches look as if they are pulling away from each other. Usually this is because your tension is too tight. When stitches are too tight, they distort the canvas and cause the canvas threads to bunch together (in fact doing this is deliberate in pulled canvas).

Needlepoint stitches should lie flat against the top of the canvas, If the canvas thread moves towards the other threads covered by the stitch,then the tension is too tight, take out the end of the stitch, move the canvas threads back into place and restitch. If the stitch is higher than the stitches around it, your tension might be too loose. Take out the stitch and restitch.

Another possible reason for this is the thickness of the thread. If the thread is too thick, it will distort the canvas. It can be hard to tell if this is the problem in Bargello, but if you are not sure, stitch a bit with fewer strands on a scrap piece of canvas to see if it looks better.

Because of the nature of Bargello, often it will look as if two blocks of stitching are pulling away from each other. This happens because two straight stitches are pulling in opposite directions from each other. It does not happen with diagonal stitches because the stitch goes over one or more intersections, which lock the stitches into place. Since straight stitches go over threads, not intersections, they are not as stable and can pull away from each other.

If you color the canvas (see the section on Needlepoint Dandruff, page 4), this will be less apparent.

Thinning Thread

Many people don't like Bargello because it seems as if the threads don't cover as well as they do in traditional needlepoint; they look thin. It is not your imagination, they do. This is for many different reasons. Here are some solutions to the common causes of thinning threads.

Stranded threads must be plied in order to change them from round threads, which don't cover as well, to flat threads, which cover better. This process is called stripping or plying threads. If you aren't doing this, it might be the reason behind thinning threads.

If it is a thread that can't be plied, switch to either a flat thread or one which can be plied. If you have been using pearl cotton, switch to floss. If it is a thread like Kreinik braid, switch to the ribbon (flat) version. 1/16" ribbon is like Tapestry (#12) braid. 1/8" ribbon is like Medium (#16) or Canvas (#24) braid. Most shades come in ribbons as well as braids.

All thread compresses some when it enters and exits the canvas. This is less apparent in threads which are fluffier. The amount of air spun into the thread makes it more or less fluffy; this is called "loft." A more lofty round thread, like Silk & Ivory, makes fuller stitches than a thread with no loft, like pearl cotton.

There are a couple of easy ways to tell how much loft is in a thread. One is to squeeze the thread, can you squeeze it so it gets thinner? That thread has more loft. A second way is to pull the ends of the thread. If the thread stretches, then it has more loft. To see for yourself compare a strand of Silk & Ivory with a strand of pearl cotton. The Silk & Ivory is loftier.

Ever have a thread which is "bent?" It curves where it came off the card or where the skein turned? Some threads which are wound on cards, may be slightly thinner where they bend. Straighten the thread and allow it to relax before stitching; with most threads this should only take a minute or so. You'll know the thread is relaxed when the curves have smoothed out.

Coverage

Like most needlepoint, Bargello should cover the canvas. But because the stitches are straight instead of slanted, it can take more threads to achieve good coverage.

I start with the same number of threads I would use for the same canvas using a slanted stitch. Then I stitch a bit of the pattern. If I like the coverage, I don't add strands.

If I can see the canvas threads along the sides of the stitch, I probably need to thicken my thread.

There are many possible ways to improve your coverage, these are some I like:

In some cases, like floss on 18 mesh canvas, just adding a couple of strands works. I often use six instead of four strands.

In other cases, switching to a ribbon version of the same thread provides better coverage than the rounded thread.

The tension of the stitches could also be a problem in coverage, make sure the stitches lay flat against the canvas.

If it's a stranded thread, ply and use a laying tool to get better coverage.

You will know that the thread is too thick if the stitches look bumpy.

If your thread is just a little too thin, think about adding a strand of floss, crewel wool, or blending filament in a matching color to thicken the thread just a little bit. It is important that the color matches exactly because otherwise these extra threads will stand out. This should only be used as a last resort if nothing else provides adequate coverage.

Twisting Ribbon Threads

Ribbon threads are simply lovely in Bargello. Their flat shape takes well to straight stitches, while the length of the stitches showcases their texture. But ribbon threads can twist. A twisted thread completely ruins the effect you want and makes your Bargello look amateurish.

If a stitch twists, remove it IMMEDIATELY. Then stitch it again using a laying tool.

Using laying tools (even your finger will work) consistently when doing Bargello prevents ribbon threads from twisting.

To use a laying tool, place the laying tool against the base of the thread after the needle has been pulled out of the canvas, bring the laying tool and the loop of thread slightly below the bottom of the stitch. Bring the needle back into the canvas, but stop pulling the thread shortly before the thread becomes taut against the laying tool. Use the laying tool to smooth out the thread, put it on top of the thread (instead of inside the loop) and slowly pull the thread taut, keeping the thread flat as it goes into the canvas. Remove the laying tool at the last moment, this makes sure the thread stays flat.

Compensation

Conventional needlepoint wisdom says that you shouldn't make straight stitches over one canvas thread. This is because with the open weave of canvas, a straight stitch can literally disappear under a canvas thread.

But in Bargello at the ends of a piece, often there are single threads to cover. This can present a problem.

There are several different ways to compensate; which method you choose depends on what will look best for your piece.

1. Make the stitch a second time – this does not always work.
2. Make sure that you are making a diagonal stitch on the back when you bring your needle out of the canvas for this stitch. By making the diagonal stitch on the back (like a Tent Stitch) you lock the intersection into place. This method works best when you must have a single thread stitch, as in Four-way patterns.
3. Lengthen the stitch. This works very well for line patterns. Your eye doesn't really "see" the lengthened stitch because it expects the established pattern to continue to look the same.
4. Lengthen the size of the project by one thread. This works especially well when you are just getting to the top or bottom of a piece.

Threads

When you stitch Bargello, pretty much anything can go as far as threads are concerned. If you can thread a needle with it and pull it through the canvas, it can be used for Bargello.

Threads can loosely be categorized into three groups based on the structure of the thread. These are stranded, round, and flat. The thread as it comes out of the package determines the type of thread. Each type of thread is treated differently in Bargello.

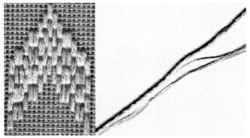

FIGURE 8: BARGELLO WITH STRANDED THREADS

Stranded threads, like Embroidery Floss, are made up of two or more easily separated strands of thread. The great thing about these threads is that you can make them thicker or thinner according to the size of the canvas. When you separate and recombine the individual strands of these type of threads, a flat thread is made, one which is perfect for Bargello. The figure above shows a sample of Bargello stitched with stranded threads. Next to the stitched sample is a length of unplied (top) and a length of plied (bottom) thread.

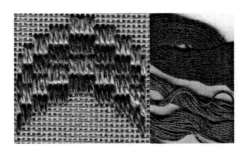

FIGURE 9: BARGELLO WITH ROUND THREADS

Round threads, like pearl cotton, cannot be separated and recombined. Of all the thread types, these are the most problematic for Bargello. Their shape makes them stand up from the canvas, making individually distinct stitches. This makes rounded threads more prone to "Needlepoint Dandruff" (page 4) The more loft (page 6) a thread has, the better it will look in Bargello. While threads with less loft are more difficult to use, matching the thread size to the canvas will look better. The figure above shows a sample of rounded threads both stitched and unstitched.

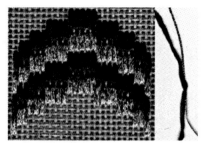

Flat threads, like ribbons, are constructed so that the thread is flat. Ribbon threads have become more and more popular and run the gamut from actual ribbons to fancy metallic and specialty threads. Most ribbons work well for Bargello because their flat texture fills the space well. They will compress at the ends though, and many are too delicate for pieces which get lots of use. The figure above shows a sample of Bargello with ribbon threads and some different types of ribbons.

Threads that Wear Well

One of my needlepoint dreams is to make a set of Bargello seat covers for my dining room chairs. One of my teachers in college had a set, in shades of pink (this was the '70s after all). I was jealous then and I'm still jealous now.

Seat covers, rugs, belts, dog collars, shoes, purses – all these are needlepoint which has to wear well. When stitched with the right kind of threads and stitches, needlepoint can last for generations. Making a rug, covering a chair, or making a belt allows you to stitch something which will last.

Or at least you hope so. Picking the wrong kinds of threads or stitches can turn your lovely stitching into a mess of pulled threads or worn patches.

The absolutely best thread to use is wool. Wool is unparalleled for wearing well, holding color, and standing up to rough use. Wool is the best choice for rugs, furniture, dog collars and shoes. Dog collars get the hardest wear. When stitching rugs or chair covers stick to this tried and true fiber. Wool has lots of loft, so even a round thread, like Tapestry Wool, covers well.

After wool, think about pearl cotton. Unlike floss, the twist in pearl makes it strong and better able to stand up to hard wear. The sheen in pearl does come off with use, so areas like belt bindings shouldn't be stitched in pearl. Belts work especially well in pearl because of their sheen and vibrant colors. Pearl is amazing for belts, totes and purses. Pearl cotton has no loft and, depending on how you stitch, may not work for Bargello.

Silk is a traditional choice for Bargello, especially for smaller items. Some of the oldest Bargello seen in museums, such as chests, have panels stitched from silk. A small Bargello piece stitched in silk is a real luxury. However, silk threads are not light-fast. The front of pieces stitched in silk which are exposed to sunlight, disintegrate over time. Do not use silk in pieces exposed to much sunlight.

Some blends and specialty threads also stand up to hard wear. Burmilana, a thin wool blend, wears well. So do linen threads. Braided or ribbon metallics, such as Kreinik or Treasure Braid and Ribbon are also strong enough for occasional stitches in pieces which get lots of wear.

It is also better to use a thread which has single strands, like pearl cotton, instead of a stranded thread, like floss. Stranded threads are easier to catch and snag.

Knitting Yarns in Needlepoint

Because the idea of using knitting yarns for needlepoint is uncommon, this section will explain how to identify knitting yarns which will work and something about the market for knitting yarns and how it differs from the needlepoint market. Often stitchers are told never to use knitting yarns for needlepoint because they do not wear well. The rough edges of the canvas are extremely hard on thread and many knitting yarns would shred under their effect. But as the revolution in fibers hit needlepoint, stitchers use, as a matter of course, many threads which were originally developed for knitting. Silk & Ivory is a knitting yarn, as is Overture – to name just two examples. In fact, there are plenty of threads in knitting shops which will work for needlepoint.

There are some big differences between the markets for yarn in needlework and in knitting. Most of these differences can be summed up by the fact that knitting is fashion while needlework is an heirloom. It has little to do with the work involved, but lots to do with the use of the finished item.

The market for knitting yarns tends towards fibers, yarns, and colors which work well for garments. And the manufacturers of yarns create yarns which meet these needs. For example, if metallics are "hot," there will be lots of metallic yarns in shops. If they are not, there will only be a few, if any.

The market for needlework yarns is more stable. Stitchers look for large color families (several shades of the same color), expect colors to continue to be available permanently, and will trade relatively fewer types of thread in exchange for more colors. Because stitching a piece can take years, or there may be a need for restoration, the needlework thread market works to keep colors consistent and available.

The selection of color in knitting yarns is considerably smaller than that of needlework yarns. Do not expect to find four or five shades of the same color in knitting yarns. Do not necessarily expect to find colors which are not fashionable at the moment. Knitting yarns come in a smaller selection of colors and, while the yarn may continue to be available, the color selection might change.

The average life of a knitting yarn is only a few years. A yarn may not continue to be available after a couple of years and may not be widely available "off season." There may be similar yarns out there, and they may be called something else and come in different colors, but keep in mind this is a market which changes more frequently.

There are probably thousands of knitting yarns out there. While it sometimes appears that a local needlework shop only sells a fraction of the needlework yarns, even the best stocked knitting shop only carries a tiny percentage of knitting yarns. Do not expect to find consistency in yarn selection from store to store.

In short, while knitting yarns are wonderful to use for needlework, there are restrictions when buying and using them.

What Not to Look For

Needlepoint is hard on threads and any yarn which is used will need to be both sturdy and relatively even in width. The pictures below and on the next page show two knitting yarns. The first one is suitable for needlepoint while the second one is not – it is too uneven in width.

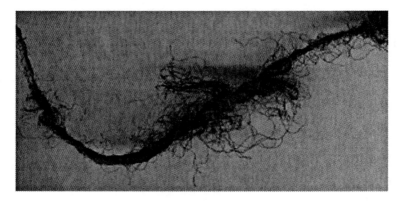

Stay away from those wonderful and tempting yarns which are very bumpy – they will not go through the canvas.

Avoid most threads which are loosely twisted, they shred easily. Some threads are an exception to this rule. Chainette threads (they look like a long line of single crochet stitches or a chain of thread loops) often work but need to be handled with care. One way to handle Chainettes is to unravel them before stitching. This makes the threads much thinner but easier to control. They may need to be doubled (or even tripled) to get a good stitching width.

Overall, there are two big drawbacks with knitting yarns. First they come in a much smaller selection of colors. Also, they come in huge quantities. Choosing them for accents or background threads is an economical choice.

Colors & Color Schemes

Using only a single stitch, in a repeating pattern, Bargello is a needlepoint technique which brings color to the forefront of any piece you stitch. The different textures of the threads you chose play a secondary role to the changing palette of colors.

Before we talk about color schemes, some color terms need to be defined.

HUE: the "name" of the color. Words like "violet," "green," or "blue-green" are hues. Grape, chartreuse, and aqua are names for colors which do not describe them precisely. Hues are either primary (red, yellow, blue), secondary (orange, green, violet), or tertiary (red-orange, yellow-green, etc.).

COMPLEMENT: The color opposite on the color wheel. Pairs of complements, such as red and green, form very powerful and popular color combinations.

VALUE: The lightness or darkness in a color. The darker the color, the lower the value. So black has the lowest value, and white has the highest one.

TINT: Lighter values of a hue, formed by adding white. Pink is a tint of red.

SHADE: Darker values of a hue, formed by adding black. Navy is a shade of blue.

TONES: Intermediate values of a hue, formed by adding either gray or the color's complement. Most of the colors we see everyday are tones of some kind.

A color scheme is any combination of colors which is used in a single project. Some popular color schemes for Bargello include:

MONOCHROMATIC: These are different values of a single color. When you see a color family of a thread displayed, you are seeing a monochromatic color scheme. Many Bargello line patterns are stitched in monochromatic schemes.

COMPLEMENTARY: These color schemes use a hue and its opposite on the color wheel. The two colors don't have to be used in the same amounts, nor do the two colors have to have similar values. I have a great Bargello footstool which is almost entirely green, with small flecks of dark rose.

ANALOGOUS: These very pretty color schemes use colors which are next to each other on the color wheel. Because the colors have tertiary hues between them, such as green-blue between blue and green, you can create Bargello color schemes which seem to transform from one color to the next almost magically.

SPLIT COMPLEMENTARY: This more complex color scheme uses a color and the colors on either side of the complement. For example, blue would have split complements of yellow-orange and red-orange. A Double Split Complement has both sides of the color scheme split.

TRIAD: This color scheme uses three colors equally spaced around the color wheel. The classic Triad is the primary colors of red, yellow, and blue although many other triads can be formed.

There are many fantastic books on color and color theory. Two are particularly good in dealing with color in embroidery. These are Mary Shipp's Color for Embroidery (newly revised), available at your local shop, and Mary Fry's Color and Fiber, now out of print.

Transitions in Bargello

One of my biggest difficulties in creating a Bargello color scheme is finding colors to be the transition between one hue and another. The key to finding transitional colors is to move as close as possible to the ends of the value spectrum (black or white).

Most of the time, this is easiest using white as the transition. In general, needlepoint threads of all types tend to have better light colors than dark colors. The eye, I think, tends to blend white into the colors on either side of it better than it can blend black. The result is that white between an extremely pale blue and an extremely pale pink works, whereas black between a dark navy and a dark burgundy may not.

On either side of white, choose the lightest possible shade of your color, so the transition becomes: light shade color 1 – white – light shade color 2. On either side of the transition you can use the shading you have worked out for each color.

If you want to make a line needlepoint with more than two families of colors, you will need more than one transition area.

The Value of Value

It all sounds so easy, pick the colors and go. But what if your chosen color scheme falls flat? All too often the problem is that the piece has colors in too narrow a range of value.

Contrast, at some level, is critical to making most things (clothing, paintings, needlework) look good. Think about an outfit – khaki slacks, a white blouse, and a beige sweater -- dull right? Because all the parts of the outfit have similar values, the whole thing turns into one boring ensemble.

But add a spark of a different value with a black belt, shoes, and sweater and see how much the contrast in values in this outfit improves the entire look.

It works the same way in needlepoint. The beauty of a monochromatic Bargello comes from the contrast in values, but if you took out the lightest and darkest colors and stitched the same pattern from those threads, it would look lifeless.

It can be hard to determine the values of thread colors. All too often the color itself gets in the way. Those two shades of pink and blue might look very different, but if their values are similar, they will look dull next to each other.

There are a few ways to determine the value of your threads. One easy way is to line them up on a color copier. Make two copies, one in color (for reference) and one in black and white. The black and white copy washes out the colors and leaves only the values, You can see the ones which are too similar.

Another easy way to determine value is to squint at your line of threads. This changes the colors so that the values are more predominant.

Quilters use pieces of transparent colored plastic to view fabrics to check for contrast in value. Usually these are red, but there are green ones as well. The red tints everything and removes most color information so that once again you see the values of the threads.

If you've looked at your threads and find problems with the values, what can you do to fix it?

The easiest thing to do is to extend the range of values by adding threads at one or both ends of the family and removing some threads from the crowded area.

But what if you can't do this or like the colors you have picked? Then you need to work on your arrangement so that it isn't too dull. If you are using one color family, make sure the monochromatic scheme is arranged according to value, and stitch using this order. If you are using more than one color, arrange each family according to value and find transition colors to blend them together. If you put two colors with similar values together, it will look flat. I know, I've done it.

A final way to break up values is to add some accent colors between the problematic shades. These colors should be different both in value and in saturation (how vibrant or bright the color is). It's also great if they differ in color. The eye will look at the accent and the threads on either side will look more like each other (in a good way) because both are different from the accent color.

Directional Light

Directional light is a characteristic of some threads and fabrics where the shade or color or the fiber changes depending on the direction of the light. You've probably seen the effects of directional light on fabrics without even knowing it. Have you run your hand over a piece of corduroy and seen how the color changes? That's directional light. Have you ever seen those wonderful taffetas where it look one color one way or a different color when viewed from a different angle? Directional light again.

Some threads also have directional light. They will look slightly different in shade when the stitch is at a different angle. Some threads which have prominent directional light include pearl cotton, Silk & Ivory, and Vineyard Silk. Floss and silk have less prominent directional light. Two types of threads which almost never have directional light are matte threads and metallics.

There are two easy ways see if a thread has this characteristic. One way is to stitch a simple Four-way pattern, so that there are both horizontal and vertical stitches. Hold the finished stitching at an oblique angle and view it from the side. Do the stitches look as if they are different colors? If so, this thread has directional light.

Another way to tell is to stitch two blocks, one of Basketweave and one of Reverse Basketweave. Look at them from an oblique angle again. Do the stitches look as if they are different colors? If so, this thread has directional light.

Because Bargello generally uses stitches which only go in one direction, this characteristic is not important most of the time. But you can use it to your advantage in Four-way patterns as well as in patterns which rotate, like the stitch in Santa's Mini-sock (page 91).

Adapt it to You

One of the best things about Bargello is the way it adapts so easily to your own decorating and design needs. Some of my earliest Bargello experiments used one accent color against a solid background or used several different colors in one thread to test out color schemes. After more than 35 years of stitching Bargello, I still find it an ideal way to try out threads. while still making something useful and beautiful

As you look through the book you will see many different approaches to Bargello. Some pieces use different colors of one thread, others use one color and a variety of threads, others combine both approaches. If the threads of one project appeal to you, but the pattern doesn't, pick a different pattern. If you want a different project than the one pictured, choose a different template or make one of your own.

Here are some ideas for making your own variations:

VARIEGATED FIBERS: The color schemes in variegated fibers are a fantastic starting point for making exciting needlework. Pick a thread which appeals to you and has more than three colors in it as your base. In looking at this thread you will see that there is a main color and one or more accent colors. You can choose which of the accent colors to bring out in your project.

For example, the Tahiti Mini-sock, page 78, uses Tahiti Waterlillies as its base. This thread has all the colors of the rainbow in it, so pretty much anything goes for colors. The two colors I chose to bring out were peach and blue. I just as easily could have chosen yellow and violet. In fact I have use Tahiti as the basis for projects accenting blue and violet, red and green, and blue and peach. The results are always different, but still lovely because of the variegated thread.

Now pick additional threads which have those same colors; they could be any fiber at all. These threads should be solid and should provide a variety of texture in order to keep the pattern lively.

When looking at variegated threads for Bargello, seek out ones which are either semi-solid (shades of the same color) or strongly multi-colored. The semi-solid threads act as interesting solids in pieces like Topsy-Turvey Pillow, page 48. or as the flower base in the Crnation Bellpull, page 76. Multi-colored threads can become the basis for almost any design. Two pieces which take advantage of a multi-colored threads to create a color scheme are the Hand-dyed Mini-sock, page 37, and the Twisting Ribbon Mini-sock, page 41.

MONOCHROME: There are two approaches to monochrome projects. One, which is about as old as Bargello, is to choose different shades of the same color in the same thread. This creates the soothing palette of designs like Big Curve, page 54, which uses four shades of one family of Silk & Ivory.

A more modern way to stitch a monochromatic pattern is to pick one color and choose several different threads. I love these combinations because, as a thread junkie, I love texture. The Moonlight and Gold Jewel Box, page 95, is an example of how this approach comes together.

When choosing different threads in the same color, aim for one or two which have radically different textures from the rest. Metallics, ribbons, and novelty threads are perfect for this.

These different textures substitute for the color changes in other projects. Depending on how much contrast there is between two threads which are next to each other, the difference can made stronger or weaker. Originally all white threads were chosen for the box, but I wanted there to be a focal point in each motif. My first change was to switch the white metallic to a whitish gold and put it in the center. This kept the metallic in almost the same color, but allowed enough difference in texture to enhance the color change. To accent the center even more I put a shiny cream thread next to the metallic. This thread "points to" the metallic. Next was linen, a fantastic choice whenever a matte thread is needed. Because DMC Linen Floss has six plies, it works well for Bargello because it can be made into a flat thread.

Cottons almost always have some sheen. although often it is subtle. Around the linen, I placed Watercolours, making a texture contrast. Watercolours is a soft cotton, so this is another texture contrast to the linen. An even softer, but matte, thread, Silk & Ivory, forms the outline. By combining textures in a single color, a lovely Bargello piece is created.

COLOR CHANGES: Changing the color is probably the easiest way to adapt any of these projects to suit your tastes. If you are using several different threads, you will need to check the colors together. This is easy to do. Pull all the threads you are thinking of using. This could even be from your stash. From this big pile, pick out four or five threads which look good together. Generally you will need a neutral (gray, black, or brown), white, or a very pale shade of the color to bring them together. If the project is ornamental, not for decoration in your home, try to go beyond your normal color combinations and pick something different. Because many of these projects are small, it won't matter if it isn't your favorite color combination, and you may be delightfully surprised with the results. A change in color changes a design, often making it look completely different.

SEASONAL: Bargello patterns have a wonderful timeless look about them, which makes them absolutely ideal to adapt to different seasons and holidays. Just by changing the colors, a Christmas ornament in shades of green and red becomes a decoration for your door for Thanksgiving, when stitched in the colors of autumn leaves. The Flames Coasters, page 89, become a spooky Halloween fire when stitched in several flame colors of Water n'Ice in a black frame.

You could even do variations to mark special occasions. Wouldn't the Sweetheart Mini-sock, page 81, be a charming Golden Anniversary present if all the hearts were in shades of gold against a cream background?

CLOTHING AND ACCESSORIES: I made myself two Bargello evening purses when I was in college. Bargello patterns, because they are lines, adapt really well to envelope bags of all sizes. They also are very elegant, especially when stitched in silk or metallics. Look at the colors of your clothing and then pick a set of threads which will coordinate with them. You can pick colors from your favorite piece of clothing and make a charming bag.

Another way to use clothing as an inspiration for Bargello is to think of the colors you would put together in a suit. The main color of the suit would be the main color of the Bargello, while the blouse or tie color adds the accent.

If you are looking for complex color combinations which can be expanded into Bargello, a great source of inspiration is men's ties. Almost any one of them from a traditional stripe to the wildest print you can find gives you lots of ideas for color combinations.

PILLOWS: I saw a picture in *domino* magazine last year of a white couch with many pillows in classic Bargello patterns in many different designs. The result was striking and completely appealing. Bargello was the theme which held the diverse pillows together, making for a wonderful patchwork of color and pattern.

You can do this too. Pick a wide range of threads in several color families. Be sure to include some pale shades and/or some neutrals. Then start stitching. You can add some additional connections between the pillows by making a main color in one pattern an accent color in a second. You could also tie the pillows together by using the same neutral on more than one item.

The broad expanse of white on the couch brings everything together. This light color accents the individual pillows while diluting the colors enough so that they don't clash.

DECORATING FABRICS: Have you ever seen a fabric you just loved and wished you could make a needlepoint in those colors? With Bargello, it's easy to convert a fabric to a coordinating needlepoint.

The process is similar to the one used for constructing a color scheme from a variegated thread. The fabric will have a main color (generally the background) and then several additional colors. Based on how much of each color is used, these colors will be secondary (used most extensively) or accents (used occasionally). Pull threads which match the colors in the fabric. Many types of color schemes can be created,

Each color in the fabric can be one of the shades in a monochromatic scheme.

Several colors in the fabric can be used together to create analogous and complementary schemes. You will most likely need to add more shades of one or more of these colors to fill in the scheme.

The background color combined with several colors from the fabric can create dynamic scheme, similar to the one in the Odd Numbers Mini-sock, page 93.

If your chosen fabric is a stripe, the process can be even easier. The sequence of colors in the stripe gives you the sequence of colors for your needlepoint. Find a Bargello line you like and translate the stripe, line for line, into the Bargello pattern. If the stripes on the fabric are different widths, repeat the line more than once in the same color to make the wider stripes. When finished, put it on a solid-color chair to accent the needlework and to set off this echo of the stripe.

PAINT CHIPS: Decorating help, in the form of paint chips which show a coordinated scheme of colors which work together, is becoming more and more popular. You can find these color schemes in paint lines of all different quality from the high end paint store to your local home improvement store. To me they are a dream come true and an endless source of color ideas.

Most of these cards have a main color and several accents. Some may even include pale colors for ceilings or woodwork. Pick threads to match these colors and stitch away. While you may choose to use the colors in the same proportion as the card, feel free to vary the colors and how often they are used.

DECORATING AND DESIGN BOOKS: Today there are many books out there made for decorators and graphic designers which show sample color schemes. Sometimes they are similar to paint chips with a main color and several accents. Sometimes you can make your own color combinations. Tools like this are great ways to try out color schemes for Bargello. Find a color combination which you like and then look for threads to match. I usually do this with floss since it is inexpensive. Once you have picked the colors, then you can take the floss with you to pick out additional threads.

QUILTER TOOLS: Quilters have to deal with the problem of color combinations all the time. Because of this there are many tools, such as the 3-in-1 Color Tool, to help create color combinations. You can use these tools in exactly the same way to create Bargello. Just translate the proportions of color to proportions of lines in the Bargello pattern.

Templates

The templates on the following pages can be used to stitch any of the Bargello patterns in this book. Unless noted, they are full-size.

Pens to Use for Transfers

To use a template, place the template page under your piece of canvas. Then using a dye pen, a permanent non-Xylene or dye-based marker, or hard lead pencil (4H), trace around the template. Mount your canvas and stitch away.

I recommend using one of the following pens. Inks and dyes used in pens change, however, so you should check each pen you buy to be sure it is waterproof and will not bleed onto your threads.

Dye Pens: Y&C FabricMate (available in craft stores),
　　　　　Copic markers - used for Manga (available in art supply stores)
Ink Pens: Pigma Micron (available in quilt stores)
　　　　　Pilot SCA-UF (available in artist supply stores)
Pencil: 4H (hard lead) drawing pencil (available in artist supply stores & craft stores)

Test your pens using a piece of scrap canvas. Color a few threads of canvas. Allow it to dry (24 hours). Wet the canvas thoroughly. Did the pen bleed? If so, do not use it for needlepoint.

Fold it into a white paper towel and allow to dry. Are there marks on the towel? If so, do not use it for needlepoint.

Only use pens which are colorfast even after they have been wetted and allowed to dry. Do not use pens such as Sharpies, which say they are not to be used on fabric. They can bleed or discolor your fabric. If a marker says it is permanent and acid-free, you might be able to use it, but test it first. Only use these kind of markers if you can't find the others.

Choose the color of your pen based on the color of the threads and make your outline thin and light. This will make it easiest to cover. If your template has straight lines, follow a thread of the canvas, not necessarily the line on the template (it is hard to get perfectly straight lines on paper).

Permission is explicitly given ONLY to reproduce these template pages for use as templates to create outlines for needlepoint for personal use only, not for resale or reuse in any other context. Other uses of these templates require prior written permission.

Finding your own Templates

Almost any shape can be an outline for a Bargello piece. While I was researching this book I saw Bargello outlines of Texas, chalices, and dreidels. The shape needs to be fairly large and free of too many small protruding areas or jaggy edges.

But how do you find shapes which will work? The image you want should be a simple outline. Just like the outlines in coloring books. In fact, kids' coloring books are the best source I've found for these kinds of patterns.

If you're not lucky enough to have a child who colors in your house, you can find lots of coloring pages on the Web, which make outstanding sources for Bargello outlines.

My favorite source of these is the image search on Google (http://images.google.com/imghp?hl=en&tab=wi). In order to narrow your search to the kind of images which will work best, enter in the words "coloring book" or "outline" along with the shape you want. For example if I wanted a Bargello mitten, I would enter "coloring book mitten" The results page shows you thumbnails of the images it's found.

If you click on one of them, the thumbnail is shown at the top of the page and the source page is shown on the main part of the screen.

Just print the page (or save the image to your computer for later printing) and transfer it to your canvas for an original design.

Mini-sock

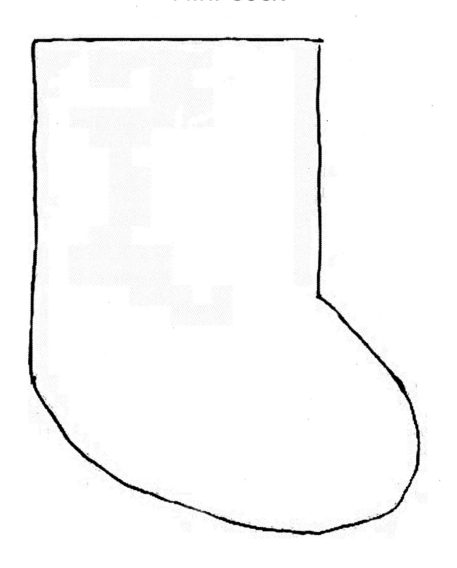

Mitten Ornament

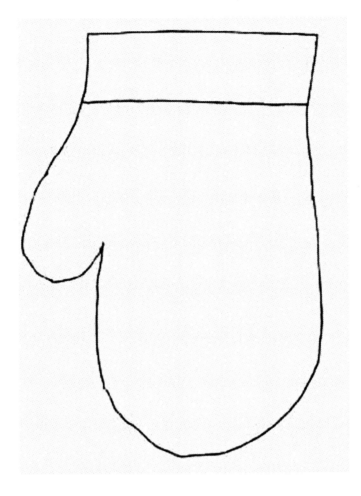

    If you are using this outline, the cuff should be stitched in a solid color with a different stitch or Bargello pattern.

Hot Air Balloon

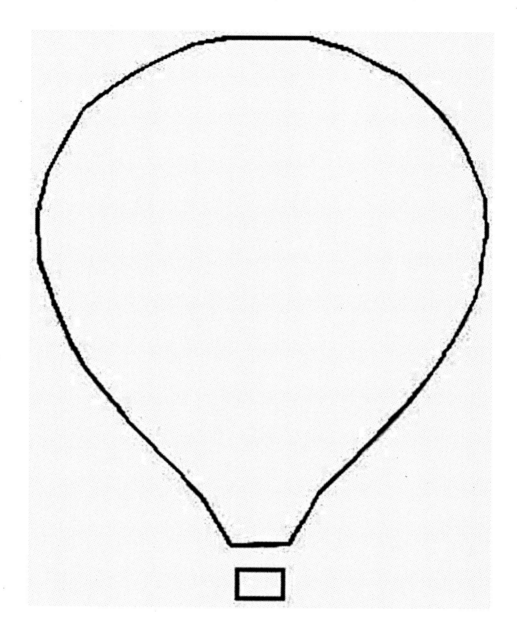

The balloon and basket can be stitched on two different pieces of canvas, and attached with thin cords. The basket should be stitched in a textured stitch, not Bargello. Rainbow Linen gives this a realistic look.

Flip-flop Ornament

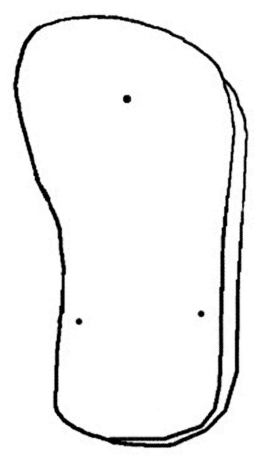

   The side of the flip-flop should be stitched in Basketweave in a darker solid color. The straps should be ribbon or braids of thread and should be attached to the finished needlepoint at the three dots.

Scissors Case

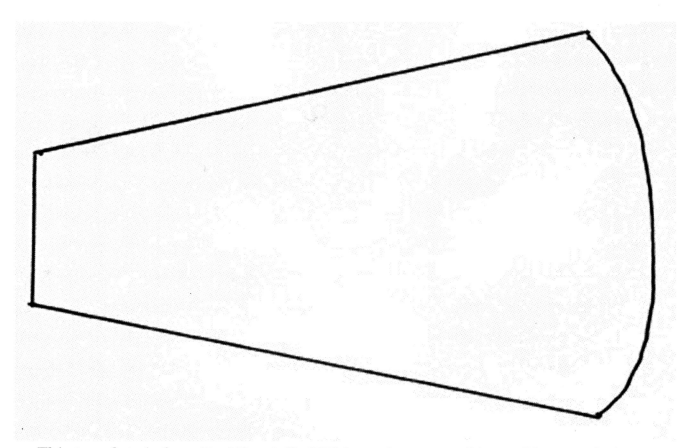

This template is from Toni Randall of Whimsy & grace and is used by permission. Reduce to 75% and trace two on canvas.

Needlecase

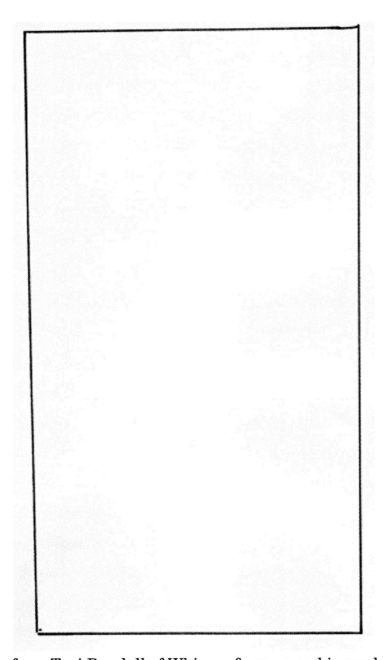

This template is from Toni Randall of Whimsy & grace and is used by permission.

Christmas Lights (stitched outline)

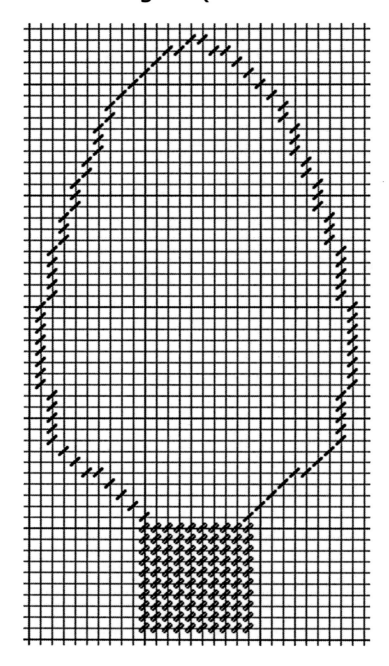

Christmas Tree Template

Easter Egg Template

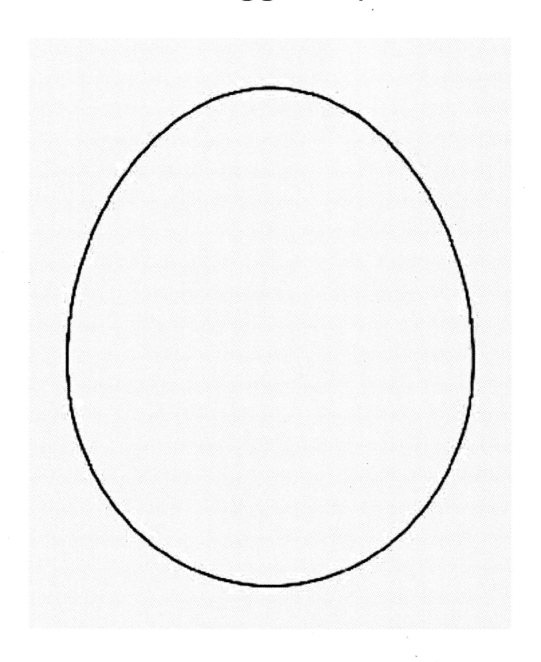

3-D Christmas Tree/Bell/Cone Template

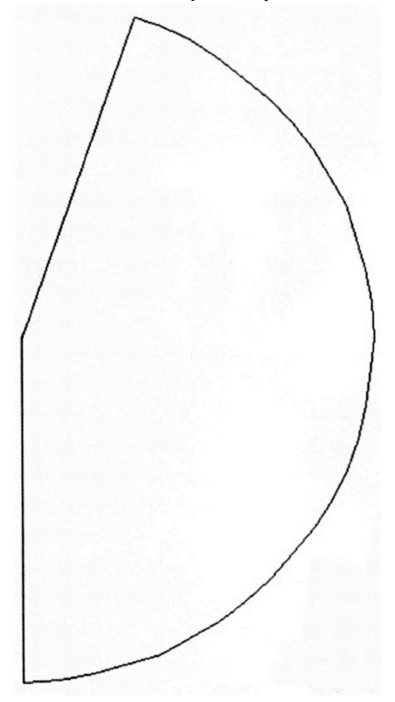

Enlarge to 140%.

Heart

Round Ornament

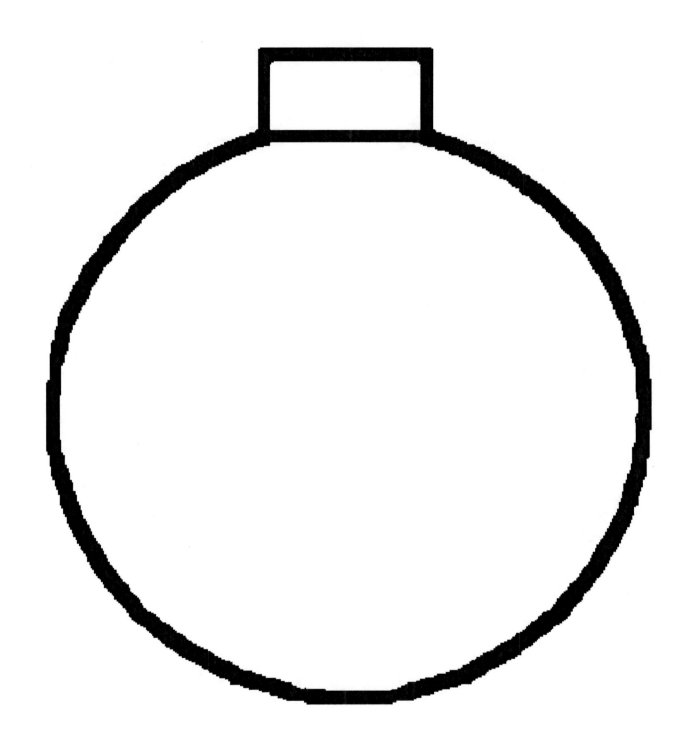

Jack o'Lantern

Bargello Tool Tote

Materials

14 mesh mono needlepoint canvas, 11 x 8 inches
1 skein each Appleton crewel wool
      751 (light rose)
      754 (rose)
      756 (medium rose)
      757 (medium dark rose)
1 skein Caron Collection Watercolours 196 Sable (dark brown)
leather tool tote in rose from Stirling

Bargello, being a very traditional form of needlepoint is perfect for this tool tote. Once completed, it can be an elegant evening clutch or a great place to store your needlework tools.

This pattern is based on an old American quilt. The curvy outline of the shapes creates a feminine look. You can make it in just about any color.

For this pattern, like all filled Bargello, stitch the outline first. These are the solid lines on the chart, using two strands of Watercolours. Use three strands of wool throughout.

Complete the pattern by filling in the shapes, following the chart.

When you stitch a filled Bargello pattern, follow this pattern:

Stitch the outlines (this lets you place the design elements properly).

Fill in all the outlines in the same shape in each of the colors.

Fill in additional shapes in the same way.

If the piece is large, follow this procedure, but only stitch a section at a time.

Cut the margins of the canvas at two threads. Remove the protective paper and place the needlepoint on the tote. Tuck in the margins using a butter knife or chopstick. Use white glue to glue the leather edges to the canvas. Weight overnight under a heavy book.

COLOR KEY:

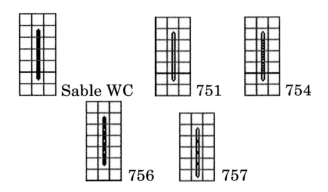

Sable WC   751   754   756   757

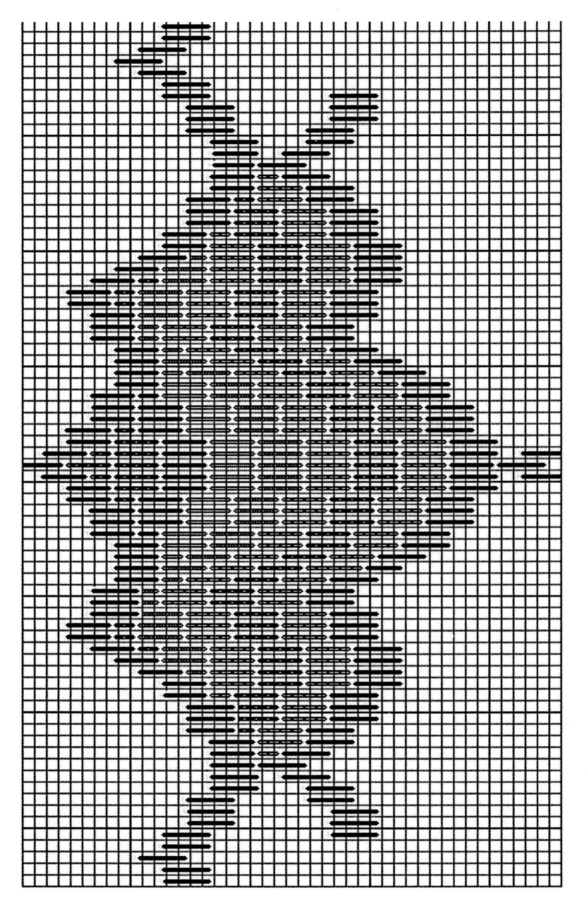

Hand-Dyed Mini-sock

Materials
8"x10" piece Zweigart 18 mesh mono canvas in white or coordinating color
1 skein The Thread Gatherer Shepherd's Silk 098 Jelly Beans (multi) -
　　　Please note: model uses another thread color
1 skein DMC Satin Floss S818 (pink)

This sock uses two threads, one a hand-dyed silk/wool blend, and the other a shiny rayon floss. It is a great way to show off an unusual thread. Hand-dyed or multicolored threads of all kinds can be used, especially if they are unusual dye lots or single skeins of a color. Adding a single line of Bargello in a solid color and a contrasting texture highlights the qualities of the hand-dyed thread.

For the best results choose an overdyed thread which has a main color and one or two accent colors. In the case of the model, the main color is violet and the accent is pink. A rayon floss, Satin Floss, is used for the accent thread, but a rayon ribbon, like Neon Rays or Ribbon Floss, would also work well. Avoid most metallics as they draw too much attention to themselves. A thread which combines a metallic with another thread like Ultra Shimmer, Sprinkles, Silk Lamé, or Ribbon Floss Shimmer Blend would be other examples of threads to avoid. Do not use for an accent any thread which has variation in color or shading, it will distract from the overdye.

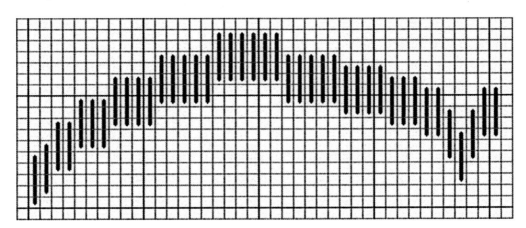

Begin stitching the mini-sock somewhere in the center of the leg of the stocking using the overdyed thread. A good way to center the pattern is to find the approximate center of the leg and put the single lowest stitch there. Because Bargello is a repeating pattern, the rhythm of the lines will reinforce the pattern.

If Satin Floss is used, use a stitching thread made up of six plies. Because the stitches are straight, there is better coverage if slightly more plies are used than are used for diagonal stitches. Using a laying tool is necessary with ribbon or plied threads.

Stitch the first row of Bargello all the way across. Each stitch in the row goes over four threads and the step is two threads.

Stitch four rows of overdyed thread, then a single row of the accent thread. When working with multicolored threads, the best results happen when the beginnings and ends of threads are matched. This is not hard to do. Stitch with a length of thread. With the next stitching thread, either thread the newest cut end (so the older end is what you stitch with first) or pick an end which matches the color just finished and thread the opposite end. Because the stocking has blocks of overdyed thread, matching is less important in this project.

I love to use this pattern to try out unusual hand-dyed and overdyed threads. Often the color combinations are so compelling, but they won't work in realistic needlepoint. Never fear, pick an accent color from among those in the overdye, pick a thread in that color and stitch away. You'll learn about how the colors in the overdye change. If you like it, pick a different accent color and thread and make a second stocking. You'll be surprised by how different it is.

Bargello Cell Phone or iPod Case

Materials

6" x 11" 18 mesh mono canvas from Zweigart in ecru
1 skein each Thread Gatherer Silk n'Colors in:
     SNC010 - Lemon Soufflé (yellow)
     SNC 031 - Soft Apricot (apricot)
1 skein Gloriana Lorikeet 166W4 Coffee Bean Dark (brown)
1 package YLI Spark Organdy ribbon 067 (apricot)
1 skein Ty-Di Simply Wool 149 (apricot)

Often when people think of Bargello, they think of patterns like this, several shades of a single color in a rhythmic geometric pattern. Scale patterns like this are great for beginners because the pattern is a bit more interesting than one which has only a single line repeated. Once the outline line is stitched, this pattern is so easy to do.

The traditional name for this pattern is Fish Scale because the overlapping motifs look like the curved scales of a fish. If you look at the pattern and just look at the solid lines (the outline portion of the pattern), you can see that it is a simple scallop pattern, but each repeat of the pattern is offset by half, so that the bottom points of the scallop meet the middle top of the line below. When you offset Bargello lines you get interesting spaces which can then be filled with stitches in different shades or colors.

The stitched area of the case is 2 1/2" wide by 31/2" threads long. This will fit a cell phone which is less than 13/4" wide and about 31/2" long. If your cell phone is bigger than this, you will need to adjust the size of the stitched area.

Begin stitching with the five strands of brown wool. Begin with the lowest stitch of one of the scallops and put that in the middle of the canvas.

Work from this middle stitch to one of the sides. Then go back to the middle and work a similar amount of thread on the other side until you reach the total width.

Following the color key, stitch the outline of the pattern, filling the entire marked area.

Once you have completed the outline, fill in the remaining dark stitches at the bottom of each motif.

Now, using the color key as your guide, fill in the remainder of the pattern with the other threads.

~Chart and Color Key on next page. ~

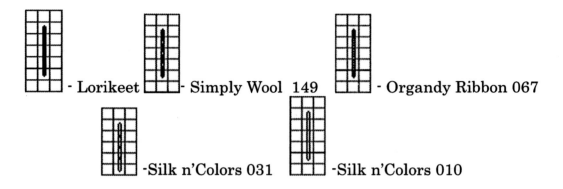

- Lorikeet   - Simply Wool 149   - Organdy Ribbon 067

-Silk n'Colors 031   -Silk n'Colors 010

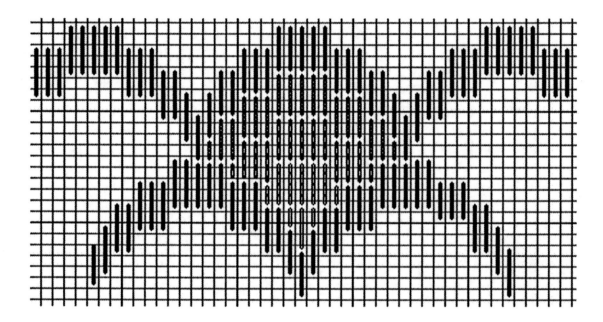

The finished case should be lined with a smooth fabric. Ask your finisher to make the case with open sides held by 1" wide elastic to help the phone fit snugly. A twisted cord and button can be added as a closure.

Twisting Ribbons Mini-sock

Materials
8"x10" piece Zweigart 18 mesh mono canvas in white or coordinating color
1 card Rainbow Gallery Bravo A102 (Iris)
1 card Rainbow Gallery Pebbly Perle P82 (teal)
1 card Rainbow Gallery Neon Rays N40 (cream)
1 card Rainbow Gallery Frosty Rays Y022 (aqua)

This mini-sock really gives you a chance to show off the different qualities of Rainbow Gallery threads. A multicolored thread (Bravo, Overture, or Encore) is stitched in alternate rows and the rows in between are stitched in three different solid threads in contrasting textures.

First choose an overdyed thread. Then choose three different accent threads, picking colors used in the overdye. One should be a metallic or a metallic combination (like Frosty Rays or Sparkle Rays). One should have a shiny texture (Neon Rays or Panache). The final one should have a matte or pearl texture (Pebbly Perle), but Very Velvet or Super Suede would also work well. The project looks better if more than one color is used for the accents.

Because Bargello uses long straight stitches, multi-stranded threads need to be stripped and laid. Ribbon threads need only to be laid. This is not hard to do. For a multi-stranded thread which can be separated (in this case both the Bravo and the Pebbly Perle), take the stitching length and pull a single ply out straight up from the bundle. Repeat with all the plies of the thread. Now reassemble the bundle with the correct number of plies for the project. In this case I used all four strands of Bravo, but only three strands of Pebbly Perle. To keep the threads straight and not twisting, use a laying tool (or finger) to keep the threads lined up parallel or to keep the ribbon from twisting. Using a laying tool is necessary when ribbon or plied threads are used.

Stitch the first row of Bargello all the way down the sock until you reach the edge of the outline. Begin with a four stitch block in the upper left corner of the mini-sock. Stitch this entire row to establish the pattern. The pattern for the project is Bravo! - Accent1 - Bravo! - Accent2 - Bravo! - Accent3 - Bravo! - Accent1 -and so on.

Each stitch in the row goes over four threads and the step between rows is two threads. Stitch all the rows of Bravo! first, leaving four threads between each row. Then stitch all the rows of each accent in turn.

~ Chart on next page ~

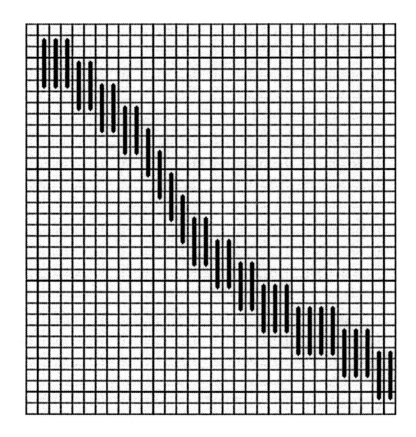

When using multicolored threads, the best results happen when the beginnings and ends of threads are matched. When a thread is finished, thread the newest cut end or pick an end which matches the ending color and thread the opposite end.

Christmas Lights

Materials

FOR ALL

    DMC floss to match thread selections

    Kreinik 1/16" ribbon in 202HL (High Lustre Gold)

    4" x 10" 18 mesh white mono canvas from Zweigart (per ornament)

CHEVRON

    Kreinik Tapestry (#12) braid in 329 (blue)

    Rainbow Gallery Rainbow Tweed RT60 (variegated blue)

SCALLOP

    Rainbow Gallery Flair F533 (green)

    YLI Ribbon Floss Shimmer 056 Spring Green/Opal (light green)

    Rainbow Gallery Fyre Werks in F34 (green)

    Ty-Di Cotton Plus from Ty-Di Threads in 340 (green)

SHALLOW WAVE

    Rainbow Gallery Flair F573 (pale yellow)

    Rainbow Gallery Fyre Werks F51 (yellow)

    Rainbow Gallery Pebbly Perle P201 (light yellow)

    YLI Ribbon Floss 043 True Yellow (yellow)

HUNGARIANPOINT

    Caron Collection Watercolours Potpourri

    Kreinik Tapestry (#12) braid 002HL (gold)

Remember those old-fashioned big bulb Christmas lights? You may not want to light your tree with them, but the outline of those great bulbs is outstanding as a place to show of your needlepoint – and a wonderful way to use brightly colored threads from your stash!

These four ornaments each use a different small Bargello pattern, which you can vary as you like. You can make them shimmer by doing the pattern all in a single shiny ribbon, like Neon Rays or Ribbon Floss. They can glitter with accents of lovely metallic threads. You could use a color of hand-dyed thread as the starting point for a combination of threads and colors. The only limit is your imagination.

Because the ornaments are small and only take a short time to do, it is easy to make lots of them for your tree.

Begin by stitching the bottom part of the bulb (outlined stitches) in the Kreinik gold ribbon. You can stitch the entire bottom in Basketweave or you can stitch it in long horizontal satin stitches. Either will give the correct look.

Use two strands of floss to stitch the outline of the bulb. This is easier than drawing the outline and all of our Bargello stitches will go over this outline.

Starting somewhere in the middle of the outline, begin stitching the Bargello pattern of your choice. Specific notes for working each pattern follow.

SHALLOW WAVE: For the ribbon floss, Flair and Fyre Werks use a single ribbon of thread as it comes off the spool. With the Pebbly Perle, ply the thread so that it becomes a flat thread instead of a rounded one and stitch with all four strands together.

Some suggestions for thread combinations:

CHEVRON: small stitches in metallic, longer stitches in pearl cotton, Watercolours or overdyed floss. Use only a single strand of the metallic. The Rainbow Tweed is a four strand thread. Separate all four strands and use three of them for the Bargello. Discard the fourth strand.

SHALLOW WAVE AND CURVE: ribbon threads like Fyre Werks, Frosty Rays, Neon Rays (all from Rainbow Gallery) or Ribbon Floss.

HUNGARIANPOINT: Use a pretty overdyed thread in alternating lines with a metallic in silver, gold or one of the accent colors. Or use alternating lines of an overdye and a silk ribbon.

The key here is to make the ornaments festive by using threads which have some shine in them, even if only as accents. Since the outline is simple, the quality of your stitching and choice of thread really stands out.

Stitch over the outline stitches you did. Having this line of stitches accomplishes several things. It shows you where to stop stitching without needing to draw on the canvas. It will give you a firmer outline for finishing the ornament. And it will mask any places where the Bargello stitches don't quite fill in on the curved edges of the ornament.

This outline is very flexible. The idea was first developed by Susan Portera and given as a free design from Rainbow Gallery. She used a variety of Rainbow Gallery threads and different stitches to make a series of lights in bright primary colors. The idea was also used for a glorious tree with ornaments in many threads and styles, which was auctioned off by the American Needlepoint Guild several years ago. While this outline is smaller and rounder than the original, it is also flexible. You can use different threads, Bargello patterns or decorative stitches to make many unique ornaments.

~ Charts on following page. ~

SCALLOP

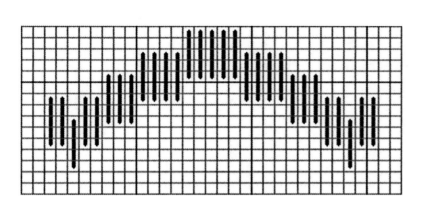

HUNGARIAN POINT

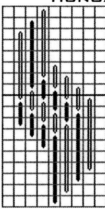

CHEVRON

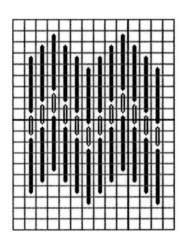

SHALLOW WAVE

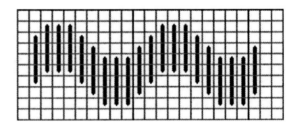

Asymmetrical Zig-zag Mini-sock

Materials
8"x10" piece Zweigart 18 mesh mono canvas in white or coordinating color
1 skein each Silk & Ivory in:

    62 Spinach (dark green)
    02 White (white)
    60 Ginger (light yellow)
    11 Really Red (red)

This pattern is a more unusual Bargello pattern because it is a straight diagonal line on one side of the point and a curved line on the other. These kind of Bargello patterns are very dynamic. This is emphasized by the contrasting colors and values of the yarns.

The stocking is stitched in Silk & Ivory from brown paper packages, a 50/50 blend of wool and silk which is very popular for needlepoint. This thread is a solid version of the silk/wool blend used in the Hand-dyed Sock (page 37). It is great for Bargello on 18 mesh because the thread expands a bit on top of the canvas, giving each stitch a great full look.

The pattern consists of alternating rows done in a very dark green. Rows of three Christmasy accents – white, gold, and red – are placed in between the green rows.

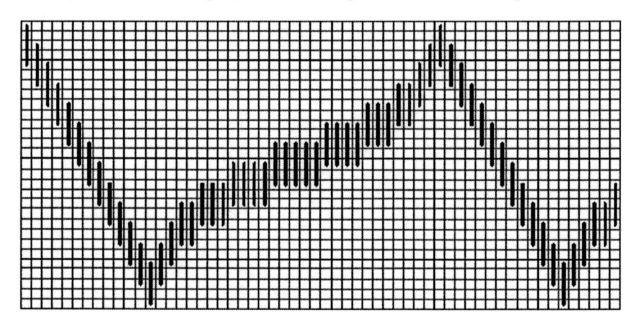

Starting somewhere in the middle of the leg of the sock, and beginning with the highest point of the pattern, stitch the line in the green thread, going to one of the sides. Then go back and complete the other side of the pattern. This establishes the line for the rest of the stocking to follow.

Skipping four canvas threads (three holes) between each row, stitch the entire stocking in the green. Once this is completed, fill in the blank lines with alternating rows of red-white-gold. I stitched this second part by doing all of the white rows first, then all the gold rows, and finally all the red rows.

Topsy-Turvy Diamond Pillow

Materials

14 mesh mono canvas, 13" x 13"
Caron Collection Watercolours, 1 skein each:
>027 Lemon and Lime (pale green)
>067 Celadon (light green)
>066 Jade (green)
>065 Emerald (medium green)
>140 Black Watch (dark green)

Other possible color selections (light to dark):
Pinks and Roses: 117 Fresh Pink (pale pink), 116 Cotton Candy (pink), 149 Cherry Cordial (muted light pink), 058 Mocha Rose (muted pink), 081 Black Cherry (dark pink)
Blues: 146 Moonglow (pale blue), 159 Silver Blue (light blue), 157 Polar Ice (blue), 150 Night Sky (medium dark blue), 156 Indigo (dark blue)

Y̲ou may not have thought of it before, but it is possible to make shaded Bargello using only overdyed and hand-dyed threads. In many of these lines of thread there are colors which are what knitters call "semi-solid" threads which are mostly shades of a single color. You can use these series of shades to make some exciting pieces. In needlework, these type of threads are becoming increasingly popular. They are often called "shadow" or "shadow-dyed."

Five shades of a color, ranging from light to dark are perfect for Bargello. Recently I did a commissioned pillow which was done with a simple Bargello line, but with a bit of a twist. Instead of being a square pillow, it is diamond-shaped. The combination makes for an extremely attractive and unusual piece.

If your stitched area is small, finish it as the insert into a larger pillow. If you want to make a larger piece, follow the instructions for creating your diamond and increase the amount of thread accordingly. You really need five shades of a color for the Bargello to look its best. In the materials list I have included lists of colors for three families of Watercolours. But if you chose to pick your own colors, look for five threads in the overdyes which are semi-solid shades of the same color. Please note that the dye lots change considerably in hand-dyed threads. My color judgment may not match yours, nor may these colors look good together in the dye lots available. In these cases, feel free to substitute different shades or even different threads to get a color range you like.

This pattern is called Topsy-Turvy because the main motif, a scallop and a zig-zag joined together, flips on itself. All the stitches go over four threads and the step between each level of stitches is two threads.

The sequence of colors runs from light to dark and back again. In the colors I used, it is: Lemon-lime, Celadon, Jade, Emerald, Black Watch, Emerald, Jade, Celadon, Lemon-lime, etc.

Begin by folding your canvas in half, either lengthwise or widthwise. About two inches in from either side, make a mark with a permanent non-Xylene or dye-based marker made for fabric (like SCA-UF from Pilot, a Pigma Micron, or a ZIG Needlepoint Marker) or a hard (4H) drawing pencil.

Repeat this process with the canvas in the other direction. Now you have marked the four corners of your diamond.

Using a ruler, draw a straight line from corner to corner, all around the piece. Now you have drawn your diamond shape. Make an additional mark at the center of the canvas so you know how to center the first line of Bargello.

On 14 mesh canvas, you will need two strands of the three strand bundle of Watercolours. Keep your third strand for a scrap bag project.

Pick either Lemon-Lime or Black Watch as your center. Now center the pattern in the diamond; this will be where the two folds meet in the middle at the mark. The middle stitch for the pattern is the middle stitch on the zig-zag section. Put this stitch in the center of the piece.

Stitch to one end. Go back and stitch to the other end. You have now established your line for the rest of the piece. Because you begin at the longest row with this technique, each succeeding row will be shorter than the one before.

Using the color sequence listed above, or one which appeals to you, stitch to either the top or bottom point. Then stitch to the other point, beginning again with the center.

Remember to use the Bargello Tuck (page 5) method for starting your threads. It gives a nice finish.

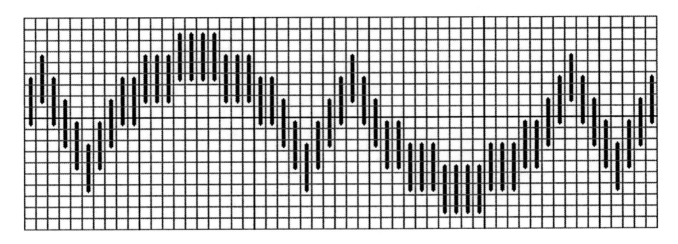

Counterchange Mini-sock

Materials
8"x10" piece Zweigart 18 mesh mono canvas in white or coordinating color
skein each brown paper packages Silk & Ivory:

      040 Caviar (dark gray)
      126 Lobster (medium coral)
      123 Crab (light coral)

This is a very traditional Bargello pattern and extremely easy to do once the outlines are stitched. The central areas alternate the order of the colors, which makes for a nice rhythm. This pattern could also be done as Scrap Bag Needlepoint™, using one or two different colors in each diamond.

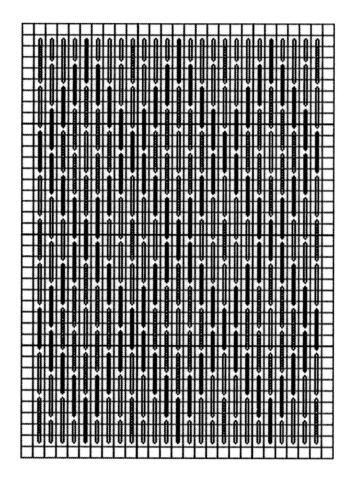

Making the outline of the pattern is key to success here. Start anywhere in the stocking (someplace in the middle or in the upper left corner are both good choices).

Make a diagonal line of stitches over four threads, going down two threads after each stitch (black lines on the chart).

Now start to form the diamonds. At one of the stitches start making a line going in the opposite direction. Continue this line on both sides of the original line. Now you have set the pattern for the outlines.

At this point, proceed in one of two ways.

Outline Method 1: If confident about counting the pattern, continue making the outline, making lines intersecting the lines you have made until the entire mini-sock is filled with the outline.

Outline Method 2: Another method to use is to count out where the colored stitches will be. Start from one of the points which already exists and then count out where the colored stitches will be until another line of outline would appear. Then start that line, make it completely and then do the same thing again. This does not fill in the area in neat lines, but it keeps filling the outline without as much counting.

After the outline is stitched, move on to filling in the diamonds. It is easiest to work with one color at a time. Pick one of the two colors and fill in the outer ring of a diamond. All the diamonds in this row and in alternate rows will use the same color on the outside ring. Proceed in this way until many of these diamonds are stitched.

Now take the second color. Do the center stitch in the filled diamonds, then make an outer ring in the empty diamonds. Fill in the remaining open spaces with the center stitch in the first color.

Alternate Method for Creating Design: This method makes both the outline and the fill, one row at a time. Make a line of zig-zags, following the chart. Including the top and bottom stitches, there should be five stitches in each leg, Remember the top and bottom stitches are shared by two legs. Fill in this row of diamonds, Then add the next zig-zag row (at the other end of the fill diamonds you made). Continue in this way, one row at a time, until the stocking is complete.

Four-Way Bargello Pincushion

Materials
10" x 10" 18 mesh Zweigart mono needlepoint canvas in sage green
1 skein each Needlepoint, Inc. silk:
>   575 (red)
>   573 (melon)
>   573A (medium light melon)
>   572 (light melon)
>   571 (pale melon)

2 skeins each Needlepoint, Inc. silk 575 (red)
1 card Rainbow Gallery Splendor S961 (ecru)

By combining a dramatic, but surprisingly simple, Four-Way Bargello pattern with a lightly stitched background and a matching pincushion lining — you get the effect of a beautiful jewel on a velvet pillow — the colors seem to float above the background.

Find the center of your canvas. You will begin to stitch there. One quadrant of the pattern is stitched at a time. You will begin each quadrant with the stitch which is at the inside center of the quadrant (the ones from each quadrant which meet in the center).

Most of the stitches in this pattern (except for the ones at the sides of each motif) are over four threads with a step of two threads.

Stitch the outline of the Bargello first, using 575 — the darkest color of thread. Not only will this help you be sure that the pattern is counted correctly, it will also make it easier to fill in the area.

Once the outline is complete, fill in the area near the center with the remaining stitches in this thread.

After this is completed, start making the curved lines which fill in the rest of the area. These go from dark (at the top of the quadrant) to light (nearer the center).

Repeat this process with each quadrant of the design.

Once the Bargello pattern is complete, stitch the background in T Stitch, below, using two strands of Splendor.

T STITCH

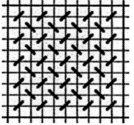

Block your needlepoint to be sure it is straight.

This pincushion is finished as a Biscournu, an eight-sided pincushion. It is a fantastic way to show off a Four-way Bargello pattern.

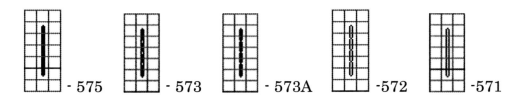

- 575   - 573   - 573A   -572   -571

Big Curve Mini-sock

Materials

8"x10" piece Zweigart 18 mesh mono canvas in white or coordinating color
1 skein each brown paper packages Silk & Ivory:

     95 Papaya (pale red)
     96 Mango (light red)
     37 Rhubarb (medium red)
     97 Pomegranate (red)

This is another traditional Bargello pattern done in four shades of the same color family. The colors shade from darkest to lightest and back again. These kinds of patterns are easy and soothing to do, largely because once you establish the first line, all the other lines follow it.

Although these patterns do not have to be centered, they look better this way. Find the middle of the mini-sock and place the highest or lowest point of the pattern there. This should be done by eye instead of counting because the stocking outline is irregular. Another way to center the pattern is to look for the middle point across on the leg of the stocking and center the pattern there.

With your needle, enlarge the hole slightly at the middle and take either the darkest or lightest color to stitch. Use that thread to stitch from there out to one side. Park the thread in the margin (without the needle) and with another thread of the same color, stitch from the center to the other side.

Now add the second color. Begin at one of the sides and go across. If there is some thread left over, park it at the side. Use these parked threads to begin the next line of these colors. Repeat the process with the third and fourth colors.

At some point the sequence of colors will become familiar. Then start skipping lines and filling them in later. The two middle colors always appear together and have either the lightest or darkest color on their other side. So if there is some thread left at the end of a line, start the next line of that color, remembering to skip the other colors' lines.

~ Chart and Color Key on following page. ~

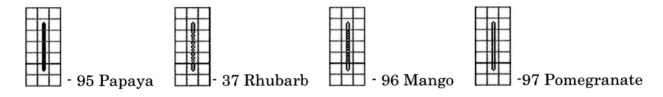

- 95 Papaya   - 37 Rhubarb   - 96 Mango   -97 Pomegranate

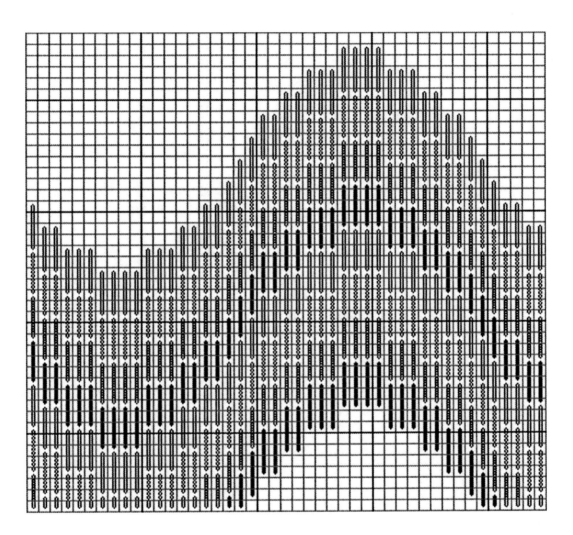

Proceed in this way until the entire mini-sock outline is complete.

Spires Needleroll

Materials
10" x 12" 18 mesh cream, light blue or aquamarina mono canvas
1 skein each Conjoined Creations Classic Stitchery Yarn:
>722P (pale turquoise)
>722L (light turquoise)
>722M (medium turquoise)
>722D (dark turquoise)

Spires is the family name for these spiky patterns where the length of the stitch is six threads and the step between them is five threads. Because of the length of the stitches, they are not hard-wearing, but they create scrumptious waves of color.

They are also a traditional Bargello pattern. One type, similar to the color pattern used here, moves from one color family to another. Because a needleroll is so traditional, a complex color scheme works as well.

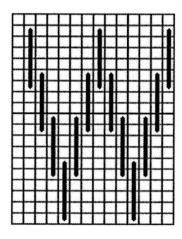

Draw a rectangle 3.5" by 7" on the canvas. Beginning somewhere in the middle of the canvas, stitch the pattern to one side, using two strands of Conjoined Creations. Park any leftover thread in the margin. Take another two strands of the same color and complete the row from the center to the other side.

The sequence of colors is dark (722D), medium (722M), light (722L), pale (722P), light (722L), medium (722M), dark (722D), etc. There are twice as many light and medium rows as dark and pale rows.

Because there is only a one thread overlap between stitches, it is very important that you stitch this pattern so that the maximum amount of thread is on the back. Remember to go from top to bottom of the stitches when the row goes up. Go from bottom to top when the rows goes down.

The stitches in this pattern are long, so it is especially important to keep the threads from twisting. This is done by laying the threads, as described on page 7. When threads are laid properly they sit next to each other throughout the length of the stitch. This makes the needlepoint look smoother and, in Bargello in particular, reinforces the up and down texture of the technique.

To finish a needleroll, sew fabric along the two long edges and trim the canvas along these edges to about 1/4". Now sew the two short edges of needlepoint together, making a tube.

Gather the fabric on the ends and secure with a rubber band, Cover the rubber band with a ribbon tied in a bow. Stuff the roll really full, so the finished roll is stiff. Repeat making the gathered end on the other end.

Your needles can be stored in this decorative piece.

It can also be filled with coins, pie weights, BB's or other heavy items to make a frame weight. Put the heavy items into a plastic bag and use that as stuffing . If you are doing this, line the needleroll first with a sturdy fabric to make it more durable.

Lines Mini-sock

Materials
8"x10" piece Zweigart 18 mesh mono canvas in white or coordinating color
1 skein Caron Collection Watercolours 145 (Carnival)
1 spool Kreinik Blending Filament 002 (gold)
1 card Rainbow Gallery Fyre Werks F2 (gold)
1 skein JL Walsh silk perle 102 (rose)

This is a very modern Bargello pattern. The Bargello lines, which are spiky and irregular, are interrupted by two lines of shimmering metallic on the foot of the stocking. It is more complex than the other patterns in the book and requires careful counting and attention to the area around the lines.

The solid lines on the diagram, next page, are all done in Watercolours or another overdyed thread. Begin by stitching the line of this thread which crosses both lines of metallic (the straight lines on the chart). There is only one row of Watercolours which crosses the lines of metallic at one of the spikes. By setting it correctly, the remainder of the mini-sock becomes easy to stitch. Start with the lowest point of the lines. Put it near the lower left (heel) of the stocking outline. Stitch this row towards the left first, then towards the right, but only to the point where it meets the line of metallic and does not cross it.

Now put in the two rows of metallic. Because Fyre Werks is a ribbon thread, it is important that it stays perfectly flat along the rows. Work slowly and hold the thread as to align it properly. If it twists, take out the stitch immediately and do it again. The two lines of metallic are four threads apart and go all the way across the mini-sock, stitch them both before continuing.

Next complete the first row of the overdye going all the way to the right edge of the mini-sock. Make partial stitches where it meets the lines of metallic and do not forget to continue the line in between the two rows of metallic.

Stitch all the rows of Watercolours throughout the stocking next. This makes the pattern easier to follow.

After making the initial row, fill in the area under this row first. Because of the irregular zig-zag, there are areas which have most of a point INSIDE the area between the metallic lines. This is correct. Work one line at a time all the way across and it will be easy to find these points. Then fill in the area under the metallic lines.

Always skip one line (four threads) between your rows of Watercolours.

Next stitch the line just above the pattern line. This line dips into the area between the lines of metallic and has a point there. After that line the stitching is entirely above the metallic lines. Finish filling in the leg of the stocking with the rows of Watercolours.

Next fill in the stocking with the combination thread. To make the combination thread (used for dotted lines on the chart), use three strands of the Walsh silk along with a single strand of Blending Filament. Treat this as a single thread.

If possible, substitute an already combined thread, such as Vineyard Silks Shimmer or Rainbow Gallery Silk Lame. These are unique threads with a strand of metallic spun with silk. Many of the colors will coordinate with the different shades of overdyed threads.

Finish stitching the stocking by filling in the blank threads. The metallic will only show through occasionally; this is correct.

When the mini-sock is done, the metallic lines form a dramatic accent, echoed by the combination thread. The overdyed thread makes swirls and lines of color.

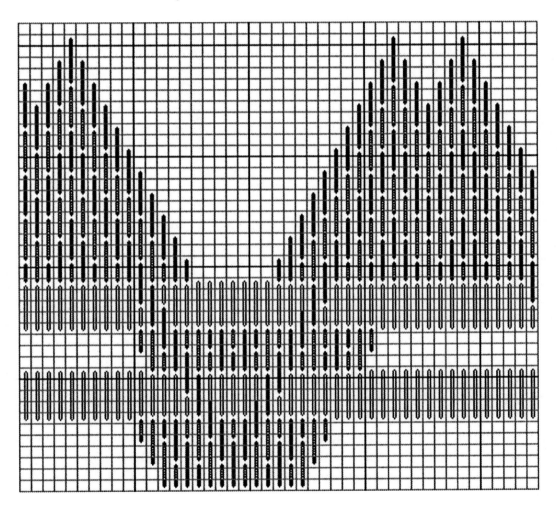

59

3-D Bargello Christmas Tree

Materials
9"x15" piece Zweigart 18 mesh mono canvas in white or coordinating color
3 skeins each Gloriana Lorikeet:
     016W3 - Holiday Green (dark green)
     016W2 - Holiday Green Light (medium dark green)
     120W5 - Green Gables Medium Dark (dark green)
1 skein each Gloriana Lorikeet:
     120W2 - Green Gables Medium Light (light green)
     121 Holly Berry (red)

By using a shape which is part of a circle, you can make a wonderful 3-D tree. It is finished by being made into a cone, weighted and stuffed. It is a great addition to my collection of needlepoint Christmas Trees.

The model is displayed on a stand with miniature presents. You can also embellish the tree with the addition of beads or tiny ornaments.

If you stitched the piece in other colors it could be finished with a handle to make a charming cone ornament (popular in Victorian times) or with a clapper inside as a bell ornament.

A more intense green is created if you use green canvas or color the shape green before beginning to stitch.

Because the pattern wraps around itself, filled shapes work better for this shape than line patterns. In any case, the pattern will not match at the seam, so keep the seam towards the back.

This pattern is a circle and diamond pattern. The pattern is symmetrical and each row of the outline has the same sequence of blocks. Each line is offset by half a pattern from the lines above and below it. This naturally forms alternating lines of ovals and diamonds. The two shapes are filled differently. The diamonds use the lighter threads, with a red accent. The ovals use the darker threads with a light accent.

Use six strands of Lorikeet throughout the project.

Filled patterns, like this one, are easiest to complete if you stitch the entire outline first. Use Holiday Green Lorikeet (016W3).

Following the color key and the chart on the next page, stitch the remainder of the pattern. Please note that the red thread is only used for the center stitch in each diamond. If you like, this could be substituted with a metallic or silk ribbon.

I find it easiest to stitch with one color at a time, completing all the stitching of that color before moving to the next color.

~ Chart and Color Key on following page. ~

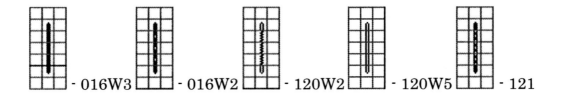

- 016W3   - 016W2   - 120W2   - 120W5   - 121

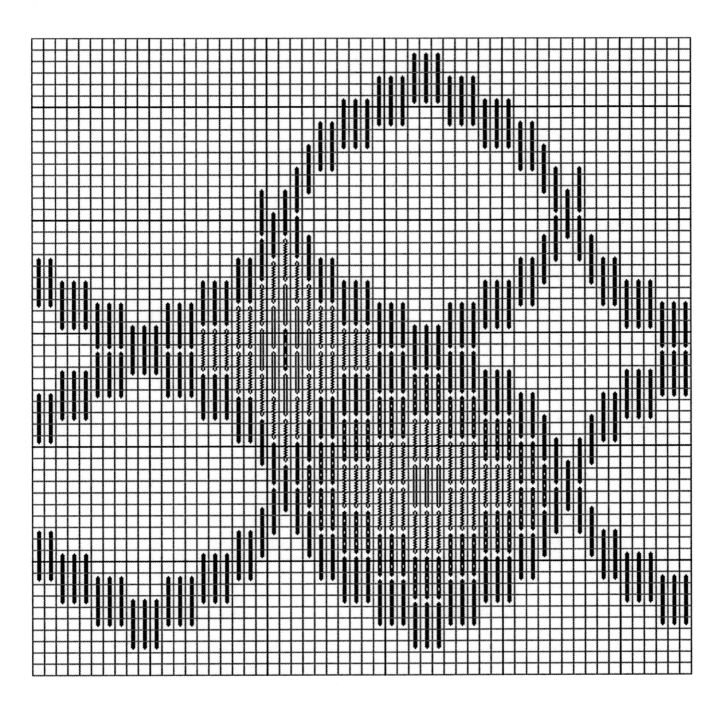

Op Art Purse

Materials
13"x16" 14 mesh mono canvas in white or coordinating color
2 skeins Brown Sheep Waverly Wool in:
     1012 (cream) light background color
     2042 (red) accent color

Another very modern pattern, Op Art is unusual because much of the piece is stitched in a single color with accented lines in a vivid red. It is stitched in just two colors. The pattern is a traditional one. It is the use of colors which makes it modern. By making most of the Bargello a single color, and "interrupting" it for just four lines of a contrasting color, a pattern looks different and more modern.

This can be done with just about any Bargello line pattern. In order to create a rhythmic background when done in single thread, the Bargello pattern must have either different stitch lengths, different numbers of stitches in the steps, or both. For example, while the pattern in Big Curve Mini-sock, page 54, makes a great background, the pattern in Spires, page 56, will not. Patterns which have enclosed shapes, such as Carnation. page 76, Flames, page 89, or Counterchange, page 50, also do not work in a single color and thread because the pattern derives from the enclosed space.

The overall effect of this pattern is the Bargello line floating against a solid color background. The look is very contemporary and takes advantage of a lovely wool thread from Nebraska.

Mark a 9" x 12" rectangle on the canvas using a permanent non-Xylene or dye-based marker. The pattern will run across the short side of the shape. Two strands of wool are needed to provide enough coverage.

Begin this pattern by stitching the bottom accent line using the red wool (solid lines on chart). Pick a starting point at the left side about 1" from the bottom. Stitch the line beginning on the left side with the "straight" portion of the pattern. End with another "straight" section on the other side to center the pattern. Above this line stitch the line of background color. Stitch the next accent line above this. Repeat the process of accent color line then background color line until there are four lines of accent color. Fill in the remainder of the pillow, both above and below the accent lines with lines in the background color.

Here's a final tip. Even though the background is all the same color, continue to stitch it in rows. It will be easier to stitch and the tension will be correct throughout.

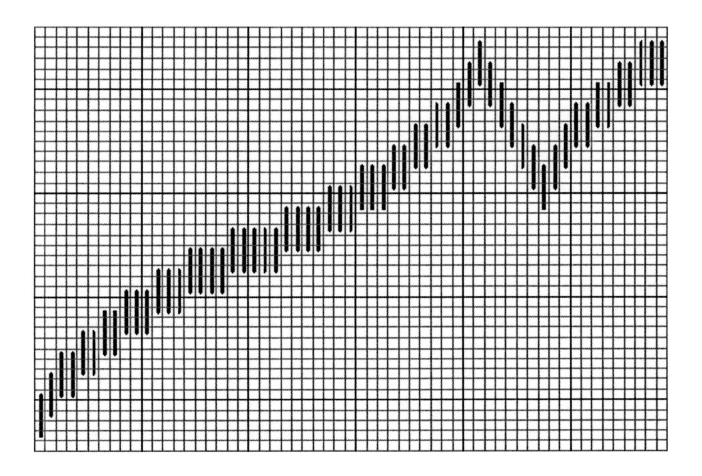

Quick & Easy Round Ornament

7"x 7" Zweigart 18 mesh mono canvas in white
1 skein each Anchor embroidery floss:
> 120 (light blue)
> 939 (light blue-violet)
> 941 (blue-violet)
> 123 (dark blue-violet)

1 spool Kreinik 1/16" ribbon 202HL (gold)

A fantastic first project, this ornament uses a very simple zig-zag line and four shades of a single color family. The top is stitched using gold metallic in Basketweave. Although the model is stitched using floss, you can use any thread you like.

If you are a more advanced stitcher, you can substitute a decorative stitch for the top of the ornament.

To enhance it more, add a little charm to the finished Bargello. Or stitch it in two color families, going from dark to pale in one family, transitioning with white and then from pale to dark in the second family, and back again. The whole sequence with three shades per family would be: dark color 1 - color 1 - pale color 1 - white - pale color 2 - color 2 - dark color 2 - color 2 - pale color 2, etc..

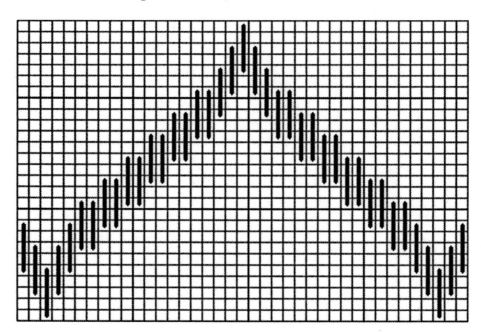

Rainbow Hot Air Balloon

Materials

8"x10" piece Zweigart 18 mesh mono canvas in white or coordinating color
4 skeins Needlepoint, Inc. silk 553 (yellow)
1 skein each Needlepoint, Inc. silk:
  414 (green)
  503 (red)
  443 (orange)
  824 (blue)
  457 (violet)
1 card Rainbow Gallery Rainbow Linen 457 (brown)

I live in California's Wine Country, where much of the year hot air balloons fill the morning sky. One of my favorites is the basis for this Bargello pattern. A rainbow of stripes is set against a bright yellow background.

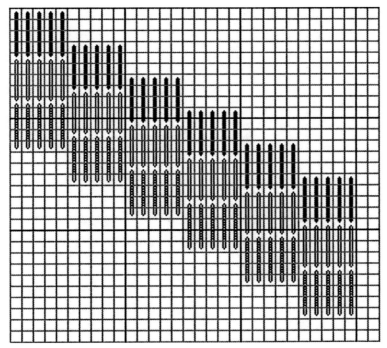

Six strands of silk are used throughout.

Beginning in the top left corner of the balloon, stitch a pattern line using the red silk. Following this, make lines in orange, yellow, green, blue and violet, like a rainbow.

Above and below the rainbow, and using the same pattern line, stitch the background of the balloon in yellow.

The basket is stitched in Double Linen using the Rainbow Linen.
Have the balloon finished as a flat ornament with the basket hanging below it.

DOUBLE LINEN

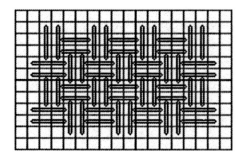

Hungarianpoint Mini-sock

Materials
8"x10" piece Zweigart 18 mesh mono canvas in white or coordinating color
1 skein Caron Collection Watercolours 032 Passion
1 card YLI Ribbon Floss Shimmer Blend 148-025 (dark green)
1 card Rainbow Gallery Flair F582 (periwinkle)

Hungarianpoint is a name often given to Bargello patterns which have both short and long stitches. These patterns are often very old and their spiked lines often move through many different colors in the same piece.

Although Hungarianpoint patterns are not as popular in Bargello today, at one time they were the most common form of the technique. In the Bargello palace is a chair covered with lovely Hungarianpoint needlework from the Renaissance.

Hungarianpoint patterns were also very popular in the 18th Century for all kinds of objects including pockets, box covers, and purses. Typically in these patterns there are extremely sharp zig-zags of color. Another aspect of these patterns is the way they move through several shades of several different colors. Modern Bargello tends to use shades of the same color most often, but using shades of one or more colors can make very interesting designs. Line patterns similar to Hungarianpoint are also often seen on the hems of Chinese garments where they represent lightning.

Because of the interplay between short and long stitches, these patterns look more difficult to stitch than they really are. This one is exceptionally easy, but lovely when it is finished. Five rows of Hungarianpoint in the overdyed silk/wool, descend from upper right to lower left. They are followed by either a row of Frosty Rays or Flair. This creates delicate interruptions while the overdye creates a wonderful play of colors throughout the stocking.

The stitches in this pattern are two lengths, over 6 threads or over two threads. One stitch over 6 is followed by six stitches over two. There is a single stitch in each step and the height of the step varies. Hungarianpoint is characterized by the large difference in length between the two stitches. It is this difference which also makes the patterns harder to stitch. In Hungarianpoint, short and long stitches are both found in any vertical column of the pattern, so the stitches interact in ways which are not easily predictable. This difficulty is most easily overcome by always working a Hungarianpoint pattern one line at a time.

Use a single strand of each of the fibers in stitching the stocking.

Start stitching in the upper right corner of the outline with a row using the overdye. Stitch two more rows of overdye on either side of it. Follow this with a row of Flair on one side and Ribbon Floss on the other.

Continue in this way with five rows of overdye followed by one row of either accent thread until you have filled up the stocking outline. The sequence of rows is: 5 overdye, 1 Flair, 5 overdye, 1 Shimmer Blend, 5 overdye, 1 Flair, and so on.

You can stitch this pattern easily with any overdye. After you have picked that thread, find two threads with contrasting textures in colors which are either in the overdye as accents or which complement it. You can see in the model the effect an accent thread with a strong contrast (Ribbon Floss) and one with a weak color contrast (Flair). The strong one sticks out clearly, while the weak one almost melts into the background, providing a subtle contrast in texture.

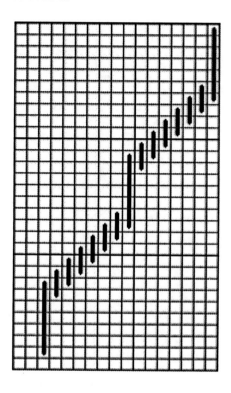

Ribbons Scissors Case

Materials
8"x10" piece Zweigart 18 mesh mono canvas in white or coordinating color
1 skein Gloriana silk floss 100 Miami Deco
1 spool Kreinik Tapestry (#12) 3509 (green)

The vertical orientation of this pattern makes me think of lines of streamers or ribbons, waving in the breeze. A narrow pattern such as this one works really well for shapes which come to a point, like the scissors case.

You could personalize it by adding a large initial in Basketweave on one side of the case. Then stitch the Bargello around it.

When complete, make the scissors easy to find by adding a fancy tassel or beaded point protector.

Start to stitch in the upper left corner of one side of the case. Alternate the rows between the two threads.

This is a very simple Bargello pattern which can work well on painted canvases. A single line of this pattern really does look like ribbons or narrow banners twisting in the breeze. A single line stitched using silk ribbon would look even more like fabric.

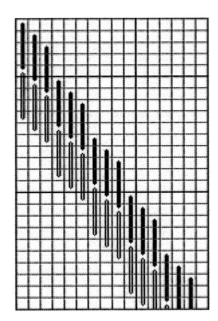

Chinese Clouds Box

Materials

8"x10" piece Zweigart 18 mesh mono canvas in sandstone or coordinating color
1 skein brown paper packages Silk & Ivory 10 Classic Navy (navy blue)
1 card Rainbow Gallery Water n'Ice WT1 (transparent)
1 card Rainbow Gallery Sparkle Rays SR36 (light turquoise)
1 card River Silks 32 4mm silk ribbon 27 (light blue)
1 skein Gloriana Silk Floss 058 (blue)
1 Sudberry Betsy Box #99521 (mahogany)

A Bargello box top is a classic decorative item. You can find boxes decorated with Bargello on the top or sides dating back to the 17th Century. In this project the classic idea of a Bargello box is combined with a contemporary Bargello pattern.

Chinese Clouds is an interesting twist on the "closed shape" Bargello pattern. These patterns generally have outlines done in a dark or light color. They line up against each other forming the overall pattern. Then they are filled in with other shades of thread. Other patterns which are in the same family are shell patterns and carnation patterns.

The fun twist here, which gives the pattern an oriental look, is that a line of the outline color curves into the center of the pattern. The side where the curve comes out alternates in each cloud.

Water n'Ice is an unusual thread. It is almost transparent. This color used on ecru canvas makes a light tan contrast, which looks great in the mahogany box. On white canvas it will be white. Using light blue canvas will make these areas extremely light blue. If you want to enhance the blue color of these areas, switch to blue (WT2) Water n'Ice. Depending on the canvas color, this will range from muted to intense light blue.

Although most of the stitches are over four threads with a step of two threads, the interaction between the outline, the curve and the filling stitches makes areas where the stitches will only be over two threads. There are different numbers of stitches in each step. Follow the chart carefully until you are familiar with the pattern.

For all closed shape Bargello patterns, the easiest way to stitch them is to do the entire outline first. In this case, also stitch the curves. Then, working from dark to light, fill in the area.

Make the outline of the clouds using Silk & Ivory. Once all the outlines are completed, fill in the shapes, using the other threads. Use six strands of Gloriana.

~ Color Key and chart on next page. ~

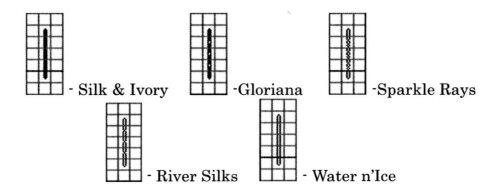

- Silk & Ivory   -Gloriana   -Sparkle Rays

- River Silks   - Water n'Ice

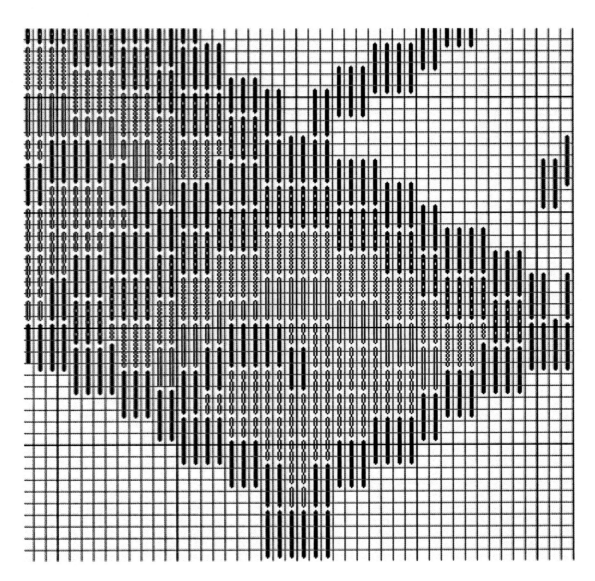

Bargello Mitten

Materials

8"x10" piece Zweigart 18 mesh mono canvas in white or coordinating color
1 skein each Silk & Ivory from brown paper packages in:

     10 Classic Navy (navy)
     127 Moon River (light grayed blue)
     128 Moonglow (medium grayed blue)
     129 Moonlight Bay (medium dark grayed blue)
_____130 Moon Indigo (dark grayed blue)

A charming and quick ornament, this little mitten is also a fantastic first Bargello project. It uses a very traditional scallop pattern and four shades of the same color of thread. The mitten is accented with a cuff in a darker color, stitched in a stripe pattern.

Silk & Ivory is used here, and can be in any family of colors. The cuff should be either a dark shade of the same color or an accent color. You can also substitute any soft slightly furry thread. Since this is finished as a Christmas ornament, hanging from the cuff, pick colors which will show up nicely against a green tree. If you want to personalize them, add the name in the cuff and stitch that area in Basketweave.

The area above the line is the cuff and is stitched in Straight Gobelin Stripe, below, using one strand of the navy Silk & Ivory. Stitch up to, but not over, the line separating the cuff from the mitten.

STRAIGHT GOBELIN STRIPE

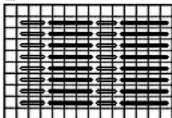

Find the middle of the mitten and begin stitching with the highest, single stitch step. Leave a tail of about half the thread and stitch the pattern to one side of the mitten. Using the tail, stitch to the other side of the mitten.

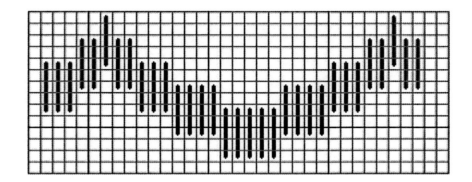

Continue to stitch the pattern, going from light to dark and then back again. This will be light, medium, medium-dark, dark, medium-dark, medium, light, etc.

To make things easier for your finisher, do not carry threads from the thumb to the body of the mitten. Finish the ornament as an actual mitten, lined with a fabric in an accent color.

These mittens are addictive to make. You could use this basic pattern and your scrap bag to make a whole tree of charming ornaments. Or make just a few and use them to decorate a wreath. You could also use them as gift ties or as packages for small treats or gifts. I'm thinking they are so much fun, I'm going to make 24 in a slightly smaller size (just reduce the size of the outline) using scrap threads to make an Advent Calendar. The numbers in gold will be on a tag on each hanger.

Free Curve Mini-sock

Materials

8"x10" piece Zweigart 18 mesh mono canvas in white or coordinating color
1 skein each JL Walsh silk/wool
       8112 (yellow)
       1655 (deep iris)
       1301 (white)
Flexible Curve, sometimes called French Curve - to make your own line

Bargello designs can be, as this book has shown, contemporary, traditional, in shapes or lines, open or closed, and can harken back to all kinds of design influences. But it is also possible to make unique Bargello designs by making the curve yourself. One way is to draw a curve on a piece of graph paper and then graphing out the stitches. This was the method used to create the curve for Swoosh, page85.

Another way is to use a drafting tool called a Flexible Curve. This is a heavy flexible piece of wire which can be bent into all kinds of shapes. Bend the Curve into a shape, then trace the shape onto graph paper. Following the curve, make the line the middle of each stitch (go up two squares and down two squares to chart the stitch for each column). This was the method used to make the curve for this mini-sock.

One characteristic of curves like this is that the slope (step) can change dramatically. This is to be expected and is a part of this kind of design. The line of this curve includes steps of one, two, and three threads. All stitches go over four threads.

Only one line of the pattern is charted, stitch this line, using the yellow thread, across the widest part of the mini-sock. Use three strands throughout for good coverage.

This line establishes the pattern for the rest of the sock. The open stitches on either side of the line are optional, they are there in case the pattern is not wide enough.

Lines of yellow and dark blue alternate with lines of white. Stitch this pattern throughout the sock. Because the step height of the pattern changes, it is easiest if the pattern is stitched one line at a time. If there is thread left over at the end of a line. "park it" off to the side until the next line in that color.

One way to use this (or any) Bargello line is to make a mini-sock in school colors. This color combination is one often found in school colors. Using someone's school colors can be a great way to make a needlepoint gift. These classic color combinations never go out of style.

~ Chart on following page. ~

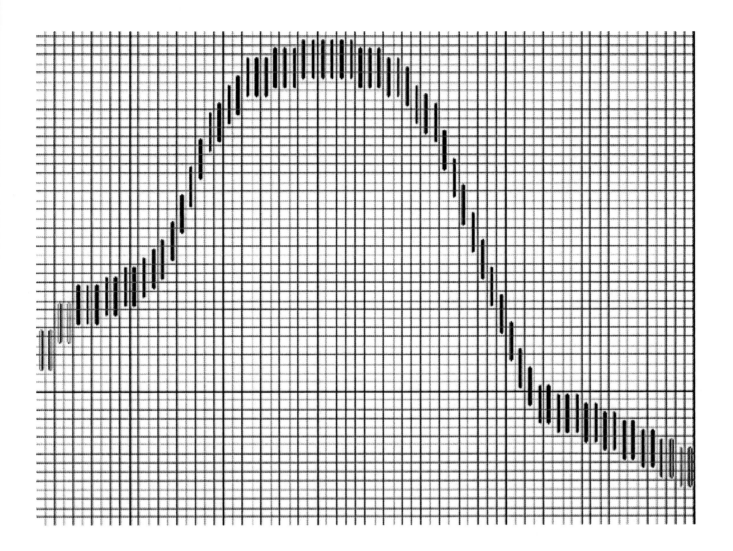

Carnation Bellpull

Materials

8"x10" piece Zweigart 18 mesh mono canvas in white or coordinating color
1 card each Rainbow Gallery Splendor:
> S987 (green)
> S1070 (dark coral)
> S898 (medium dark coral)
> S912 (light coral)
> S805 (pale coral)

2 skeins Northern Lights Silk 034 Medium Jade (green)
5" brass or wood bellpull hardware

Carnations, with their distinctive petals have been an inspiration for Bargello for Centuries. One of the flower's common names is "pinks." From this we get "pink" the color. "Pinking shears" are called this because the edges of carnations are pinked, from their common name, and so the scissors which make the same cut have been given this name.

This very traditional pattern make a delightful bellpull. The base of each flower is green, while the petals are shaded in various colors of coral. While the flowers could be any color, I like this slight variation on the traditional.

Use six strands of silk throughout. Be sure to separate and recombine the threads for best coverage.

Using a permanent non-Xylene or dye-based marker, mark a 4 1/4" by 6 1/4" rectangle on the canvas. The extra quarter inch will make the edges of the bellpull look finished.

Following the color key below, stitch the carnation. Begin by outlining each motif using the green Splendor. Once the outline is complete, you can either begin with the flowers themselves or with the green bases.

After the needlepoint is stitched and blocked, finish the bellpull.

COLOR KEY:

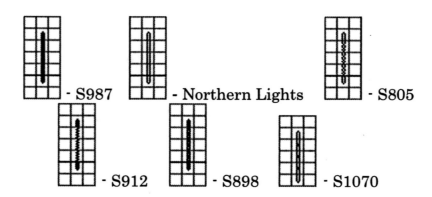

- S987   - Northern Lights   - S805

- S912   - S898   - S1070

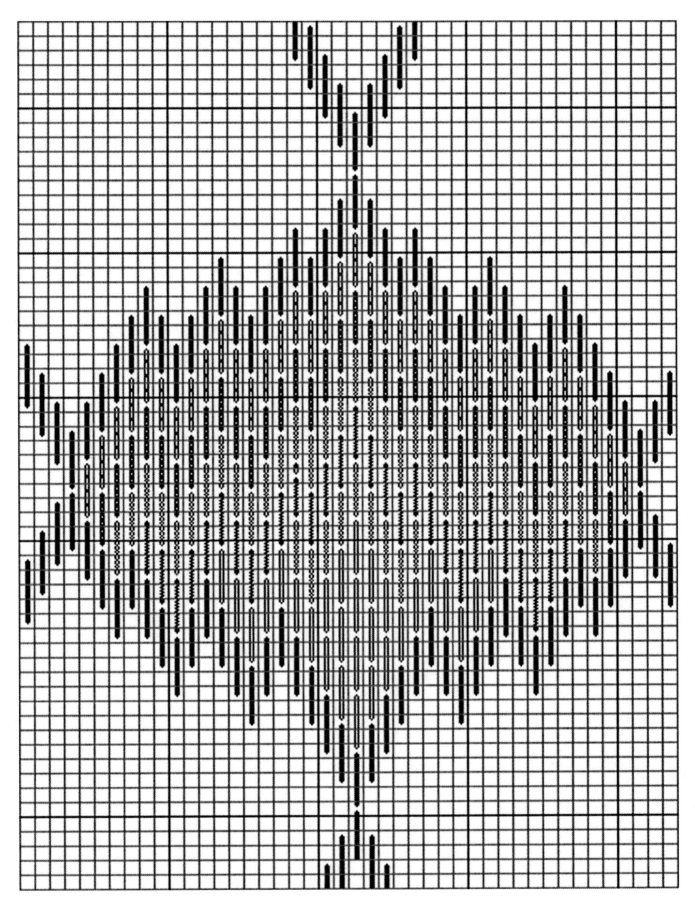

Tahiti Mini-sock

Materials
8"x10" piece Zweigart 18 mesh mono canvas in white or coordinating color
1 skein Waterlillies silk from Caron Collection Tahiti
2 spools Kreinik Medium (#16) braid or other metallic thread, to match
1 skein matte thread, such as Rainbow Gallery Pebbly Perle
1 skein embroidery floss

This mini-sock has a graceful curve, which looks like the arches of a Gothic church. This curve is caused by using two different steps in the pattern. At the top of the arch the step is only one thread, while the step is two threads along the sides. There is only one stitch in each step.

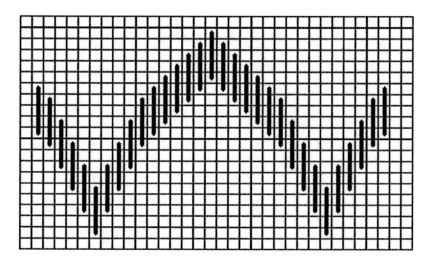

Begin stitching a single line of the pattern, using the silk (four strands). Begin in approximately the middle of the stocking. The pattern continues on either side. Stitch the entire row across. The row forms the base of your pattern.

Now start stitching the other rows. The order of the colors and fibers is: Waterlillies, Pebbly Perle, Metallic #1, Waterlillies, Floss, Metallic #2, Waterlillies, Pebbly Perle, etc.

Continue stitching the rows in the established order until you have filled in the entire stocking is complete.

Pink of Perfection Heart

Materials

7"x8" piece Zweigart 18 mesh mono canvas in white or coordinating color
1 skein each Needlepoint, Inc. Northern Lights overdyed silk
        064 Baby Pink (pale pink)
        069 Burnt Umber (dark red)
2 skeins each Needlepoint, Inc. Northern Lights overdyed silk
        065 Ol d Rose (light pink)
        056 Harmony (dark pink)
        067 Old Gingo (red)
1 Mill Hill Treasures 13047 Large Heart Crystal AB

It is close to Valentine's Day as I write this and I am thinking pink. It's one of my favorite colors, so I hardly need that excuse. This design uses a simple heart outline and a dramatic series of threads, ranging from pink to red and back, to create a lovely Valentine.

Trace the heart shape onto the canvas using a permanent non-Xylene or dye-based marker.

This Bargello line is unusual in that the pattern is vertical, not horizontal. The sequence of the threads will be: pale pink (064) - light pink (065) - dark pink (056) - red (067) - dark red (069) - red (067) - dark pink (056) - light pink (065) - pale pink (064) and so on.

Once the Bargello is complete, embellish it with ribbon flowers, charms, buttons, or beads. The model uses a crystal heart from Mill Hill.

~ Chart on following page. ~

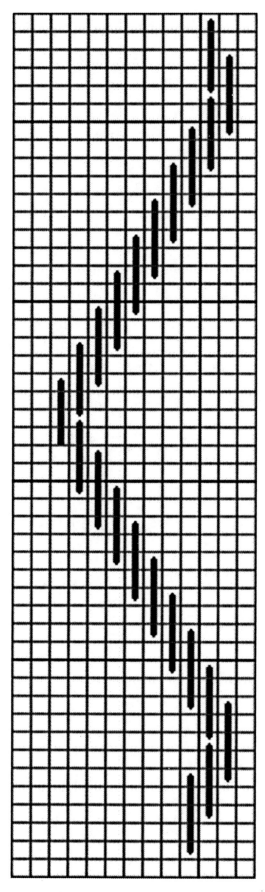

Sweetheart Mini-sock

Materials

8"x10" piece Zweigart 18 mesh mono canvas in white or coordinating color
Crewel-weight wool in light pink for the background
Assorted pink, salmon and red threads from your stash, such as:
>Fyre Werks in red and pink
>Overdyed threads in dark red
>Rhapsody in pink to yellow (R01) (cut out yellow parts)
>Sampler Threads in Victorian Pink (cut out gold part, if present)
>Needlepoint, Inc. silk in bright red
>Flower Thread in salmon
>Neon Rays in pink and salmon

At least eight different scrap threads (i.e. threads from your stash) should be used in the hearts for this project. Choose a range of textures – the excitement of the pattern comes from the play of textures and colors. However, do not choose too many metallics and shiny threads. These tend to draw attention to themselves and should be used either sparingly or as the only fiber.

Try to keep the colors for the hearts on the light side. This is especially important with dark background colors. The dark colors in the hearts also draw attention to themselves and should also be used sparingly.

This is a monochromatic color scheme done in a small space. It is also possible to make this pattern less restrictive in color. Red is between violet and orange on the color wheel. Instead of the colors in the model, which tend towards salmon (red-orange), they could easily have tended towards fuchsia/burgundy (red-violet). Pull both kinds of threads from stash, although you may end up only using one.

Make sure the background color is one which will harmonize with all the scrap threads, but not be dominant. A pale pink reinforces the overall color scheme, but is still a background. White would have looked harsh and red would have been too overwhelming.

Beginning someplace near the center of the outline and start to stitch the background (solid black lines on the chart). Use three strands of crewel wool on 18 mesh. This makes for a nice, full background. Stitch the entire background.

Begin filling in the hearts. Each heart has two colors in it. Never using the same combination, these are filled from your assortment of red and pink threads. Choosing the colors becomes easier by following some simple rules:
>Begin with a base color (in this case it was the red silk).
>Pick a random heart to begin stitching
>Decide whether the top or the bottom of this heart will use this thread.
>Pick a second thread in a different texture and color for the other line of stitching.

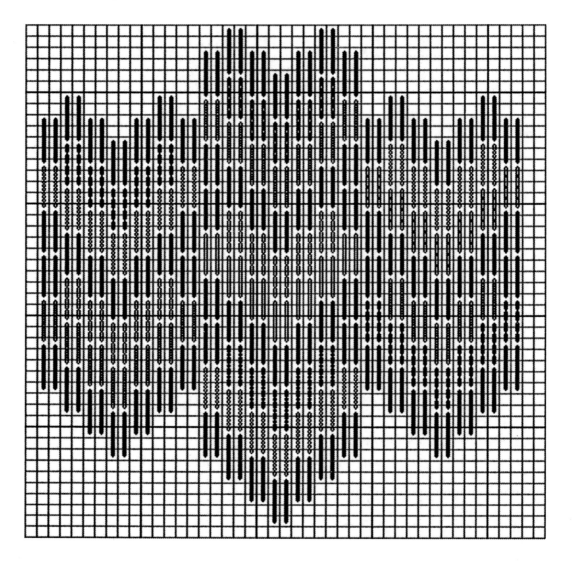

Stitch the heart and repeat the process with another heart. Try not to put the same thread in the same position (top or bottom line) in two adjacent hearts.

Dots Coin Purse

Materials
8"x10" piece Zweigart 18 mesh mono canvas in white or coordinating color
2 cards Rainbow Gallery Fyre Werks Soft Sheen FT113 (black)
scraps of threads in many different bright colors
Lee's Needle Arts Card Case or Needlepoint of Back Bay Coin Purse in black

Scrap Bag Needlepoint™ is my name for needlepoint done with all those bits and pieces of thread you have in your stash. This pattern (and Sweetheart, page 81) are both designs which use what you have to make charming needlepoint.

In Scrap Bag Needlepoint™, you want a look which is unplanned, so do not put two diamonds of the same texture or color next to each other. Some threads, like metallics and overdyes, draw attention to themselves, so either make them the dominant texture or use them sparingly.

Using a permanent non-Xylene or dye-based marker, trace a rectangle, slightly larger than the opening for the coin purse. The rectangle for this card case is 5 1/8" x 4 3/8".

The outline is stitched using the metallic ribbon. A laying tool will help you keep the thread from twisting. Stitch the outline first and then fill in the centers with two colors from your scrap bag. Try not to use the same two colors in the same order for more than one center; this helps preserve the scrappy look. Lots of metallics, velours, rayons, and silks will help make the purse look more formal.

Because the outline is metallic ribbon, this is not an accessory for everyday use, I would use it in an evening bag to carry those few things you need.

Using your scraps to make a Bargello piece which has small filled areas is tremendous fun. You never know what the design will look like, but they are always lovely. On the next page, under the Dots pattern, I have included a second Bargello pattern, reproduced from my book Scrap Bag Needlepoint. It is called Stained Glass and is one of my favorite patterns.

~Charts on next page. ~

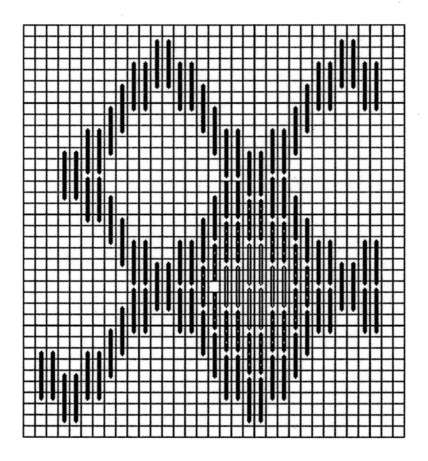

STAINED GLASS

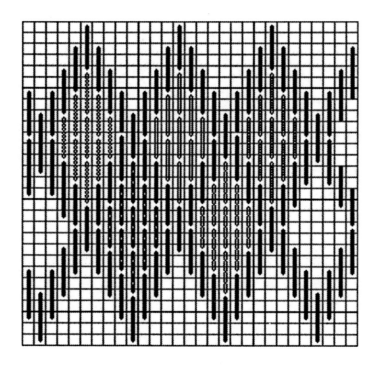

Swoosh Mini-sock

Materials
8"x10" piece Zweigart 18 mesh mono canvas in white or coordinating color
1 skein each DMC embroidery floss in:
>437 (pale golden brown)
>436 (light golden brown)
>435 (golden brown)
>434 (medium golden brown)
>791 (cobalt)

Diagonal Bargello is simple to explain. It uses Bargello patterns, but all the stitches are diagonal (going over intersections instead of threads) instead of straight. This makes them challenging to stitch and also causes the lines to move in interesting ways. A characteristic of Bargello is that the lines move in either zig-zags (straight diagonals) or scallops (curves). Diagonal Bargello moves in almost straight lines or extremely shallow curves. Some Diagonal Bargello patterns look as if they are loosely curled ribbons hanging from the top of the piece. Other pieces (Hungarianpoint done with diagonal stitches) move in almost straight lines across the canvas.

Diagonal Bargello is not well known but worth exploring. Most of the line patterns in the book and simple shape patterns (Sweetheart and Counterchange) could be converted to diagonal Bargello. However, before committing to a piece, even as small as a mini-sock, stitch a line of the pattern on a scrap piece of canvas. Often when the pattern is turned, it is not as pleasing as it was originally.

The unusual color scheme of this mini-sock is inspired by California's golden hills. The gold colors look like the grass on the hills in late summer, while the deep blue accent is inspired by a summer sky. To use a different color scheme, pick four shades of the main color and then an accent shade in a color which is close to the complement of the main color. Because Diagonal Bargello has such an unusual shape, do not use metallic threads for this design.

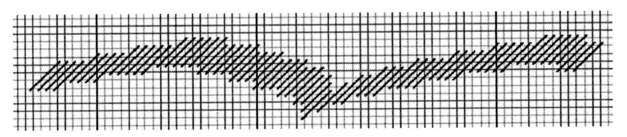

This pattern is a simple curve (charted on previous page). The number of stitches in each step is 1, 1, 2, 3, 4, 5, 6, 5, 4, 3, 2, 1, 1. It can be a little hard to tell from the graph. Each stitch goes over three intersections diagonally from the starting point. The next step begins in the square that is in the middle of the previous stitch, along the next diagonal.

Begin stitching near the bottom of the stocking "leg" with the blue line. Begin with the first single stitch step in the center. Working with diagonal instead of straight stitches in Bargello patterns can be somewhat confusing at the start, so do the first line slowly. Remember, each stitch goes over three squares (four intersections) diagonally from the starting point. Once the pattern is established the work goes fairly quickly, as each new row is the same.

You may have come across Diagonal Bargello patterns before and not recognized them. A lovely textured needlepoint stitch called Diane's Lace, below, is really a Diagonal Bargello pattern. Usually it is stitched in only a single color, but try it in a range of colors and you will see some lovely Bargello.

DIANE'S LACE

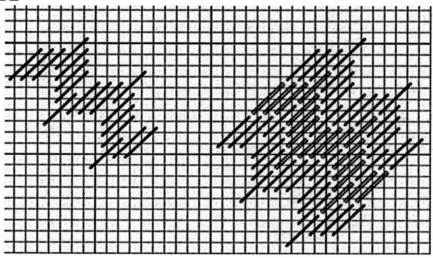

Scrolls Tote Bag

9"x9" Zweigart 14 mesh mono canvas in white
1 skein each Appleton crewel wool
     942 (light pink)
     944 (pink)
     946 (dark pink)
2 skeins Appleton crewel wool 328 (navy)
1 Patti Paints Tote Bag or other tote bag

Any tote bag can be embellished easily with needlepoint, and Bargello makes a particularly attractive option. Begin by stitching the Bargello. Following the stitching instructions, you will find instructions to finish the tote bag yourself, using a few simple supplies.

The tote bag pictured is from Patti Paints, a needlepoint designer. While this bag is no longer available, this company has many other totes and purses which make excellent showcases for your stitching. You can also buy a tote bag at any store and embellish it. Finally several companies such as Needlepoint of Back Bay and Lee NeedleArts make bags and totes ready to self-finish.

This unusual Bargello pattern was developed by Dorothy Kaestner. Although she is best known for Four-way Bargello, she designed many lovely patterns. This pattern, Scrolls, is stitched in three shades of pink crewel wool. The pattern does not intersect, although the individual scrolls touch, making a gentle, sloping line of motifs. There is open background between the scrolls. It can be stitched in a number of ways: Bargello Stitches, Basketweave, Pattern Darning, or Brick Stitches.

Begin by drawing a 5" square on your canvas.

On the chart only one complete scroll is shown, the other scrolls show with only a few stitches shown for placement.

Begin to stitch somewhere in the middle of the square and completely stitch the first scroll. Referring to the chart for placement, stitch a second scroll. Continue in this way, stitching each scroll completely, until the square is filled. Use three strands throughout.

Finish the project by stitching the background using three strands of navy (328) crewel wool. Brick Stitch is most effective here. The Brick Stitches should be over two threads and should have two stitches in each step. They should be vertical, like the Bargello stitches.

Block the needlepoint and trim it so that there is a 5 thread margin. Cut a piece of SkirTex (a thick underfacing for upholstery) or plastic canvas, just slightly smaller than the stitched area. Place this on the back side of the canvas.

Trim the corners and turn the margins under. Enclosing the lining. Glue and let dry by placing a heavy weight on it.

Using a hot glue gun, attach the canvas to the side of the tote. You could also find a pretty trim and hot glue it around the edges to make a pretty finish.

That's it – you're done!

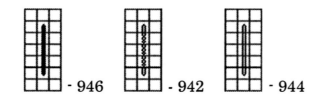

- 946   - 942   - 944

Flames Coasters

Materials

14-mesh mono canvas 12 inches x 12 inches
Sudberry House Walnut Coasters 95031
1 ounce each Brown Sheep Waverly Wool
      5061 (dark green)
      5063 (medium green)
      5065 (light green)
      2042 (red)
1 skein brown paper packages Silk & Ivory 02 (white) or
      12 ounce Waverly wool 1001 (white)

Another traditional pattern, flames. often has an area at the bottom of each diamond which is stitched in red, representing the flame. The remainder of the diamond is filled with monochromatic colors, shading from light at the bottom to dark at the edges. The outline can be either the darkest shade of this color or an accent color.

Line patterns and small closed Bargello patterns are outstanding for coasters.

Begin by using a permanent non-Xylene or dye-based marker to trace four 3.5" x 3.3" outlines on a piece of canvas. Separate each outline by about 1". The four coasters will fit onto one piece of canvas. If you would prefer to stitch each coaster on a separate piece of canvas, cut four 7" x 7" pieces of canvas.

Waverly Wool is a Persian Wool from a company in Nebraska. It is a soft wool and comes in a wonderful range of colors. Some of the color families have as many as seven shades in them. The three strands of this wool are all even and it is easy to ply. For Bargello, two strands cover beautifully on 14 mesh canvas.

Wool is a wonderful fiber for coasters. It wears well, it is naturally water-resistant, and it has a springiness which makes for great padding. Don't be afraid to use wool for this project – you'll be delighted with the results.

Silk & Ivory or Waverly Wool can be used for the white. The silk in this blend adds a pleasant bit of extra texture, while still preserving a wooly look.

To finish your coasters, begin by cutting four squares of plastic canvas just slightly smaller than the finished coasters. The plastic canvas is waterproof and can be used easily to make the coasters.

Cut out each coaster and trim the margin to about 1/2".

Turn the edges of the canvas to the back and glue them down..

Let it dry, weighted with a heavy book, overnight.

Put glue on the inside of the coasters and place the dried needlepoint on it. Turn them upside down and weight them to dry.

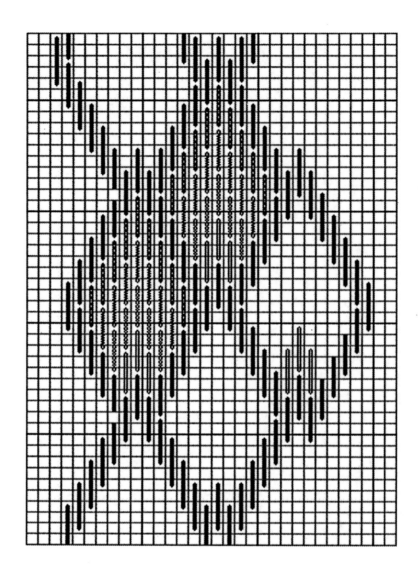

90

Santa's Mini-sock

Materials
18-mesh mono canvas 6 inches x 8 inches
2 skeins brown paper packages Silk & Ivory 93 Red Hot (red)
1 skein brown paper packages Silk & Ivory 02 White (white)

This pattern, called Interlocked Chevrons, may not look much like Bargello, but it is related to Four-way Bargello in that the pattern moves around a center in each of four directions. But it is much easier to do than Four-way Bargello. Finding the rhythm of the stitch is easy. In a single color of thread with a directional sheen, like Silk & Ivory, it takes on a wonderful damask look, because the color looks slightly different in the vertical stitches than in the horizontal ones.

This stocking gives you the rich look of Santa's suit with the look of the red velvet and white fur, so it has a cuff and allows the beauty of this stitch to show through.

This idea, of using a single attractive stitch or needlepoint pattern, is a wonderful way to try out a new stitch or new thread and make an ornament. The pattern you pick should be sufficiently large and/or complex to hold the viewer's interest for the entire piece; small stitches and patterns will not work well. Adding a cuff or border in another color or stitch also makes the mini-sock look more finished. You could also use this as a way to try out some background ideas instead of a doodle cloth.

The lush look for the ornament comes from using heavier-weight threads on 18 mesh canvas. Although it does not look as if they will, many threads of this type work well on this smaller size canvas because they can compress nicely to fit. You may have to use a slightly larger size of needle to stitch with ease. Some threads which will work include Appleton and other types of tapestry wool, Silk N' Cream, Backgrounds, and Lorikeet.

With a permanent non-Xylene or dye-based marker, make a small mark at one side for the cuff about 1" down from the top of the mini-sock. The cuff size is approximate, as you should end the body of the mini-sock with a complete motif, so there is no compensation.

Beginning somewhere in the middle of the mini-sock, start making the Chevron motif, using the red Silk & Ivory. Only do the Florentine parts of the motif, the centers, in Brick Stitch, will be filled in later.

If you look at the graph, you will see that a single motif is made up of four interlocking patterns, which rotate around a center section. These motifs meet others on the sides. Where two motifs meet, there is a cross of four stitches. Noticing this really helps to place the motifs. When stitching this pattern, begin each new motif with one of the arms of this cross and work around in a circle. Although the pattern is fairly straightforward, it can be tricky, so I ALWAYS refer to the diagram as I stitch.

Continue making the motifs all over the stocking. Once you have made all the motifs, you can begin to fill the centers. There are two kinds of centers both done in Brick Stitch.

The centers of the single motifs are done in Vertical Brick Stitch. The areas between motifs are done in Horizontal Brick Stitch. To keep from getting confused, I did all the centers of one type at the same time.

Now you are ready to stitch the cuff, which is done in a simple one stitch up-one stitch down Florentine pattern, which could also be called Giant Vertical Brick Stitch. Use the white silk & Ivory for the cuff.

As a last touch, make the cuff furry, so brush it, using an index card to cover the body of the stocking so you will not accidentally brush it as well.

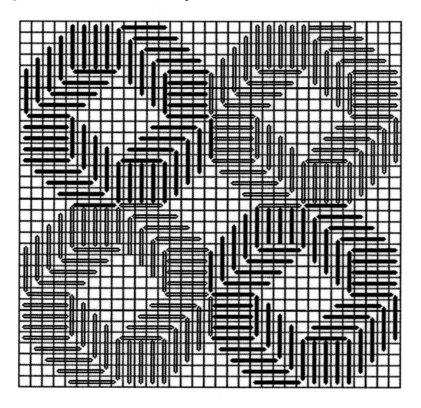

INTERLOCKING CHEVRONS CENTERS   **GIANT VERTICAL BRICK**

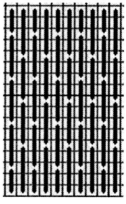

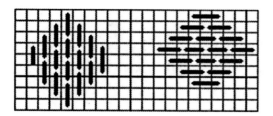

Odd Numbers Mini-sock

8"x10" Zweigart 18 mesh mono canvas in white
1 skein each brown paper packages Silk & Ivory
    02 White (white)
    20 Teal (blue-green)
    75 Pansy (blue-violet)

I know it sounds like an odd name for a pretty zig-zag design, but each of the lines in the pattern has an odd number of steps. It uses an analogous color scheme of blue-green and blue-violet, enlivened by white. Because the pattern is so busy with its many changes of direction, stick to solid colors and plenty of a neutral to make the lines stand out.

The pattern is dramatic and takes up most of the width of the mini-sock, so begin the pattern with the highest point in the upper left corner of the sock, using the blue-green thread. Stitch one line as the pattern line, then stitch the other lines in this sequence: blue-green, white, blue-violet, white, blue-green, etc.

~ Chart on next page. ~

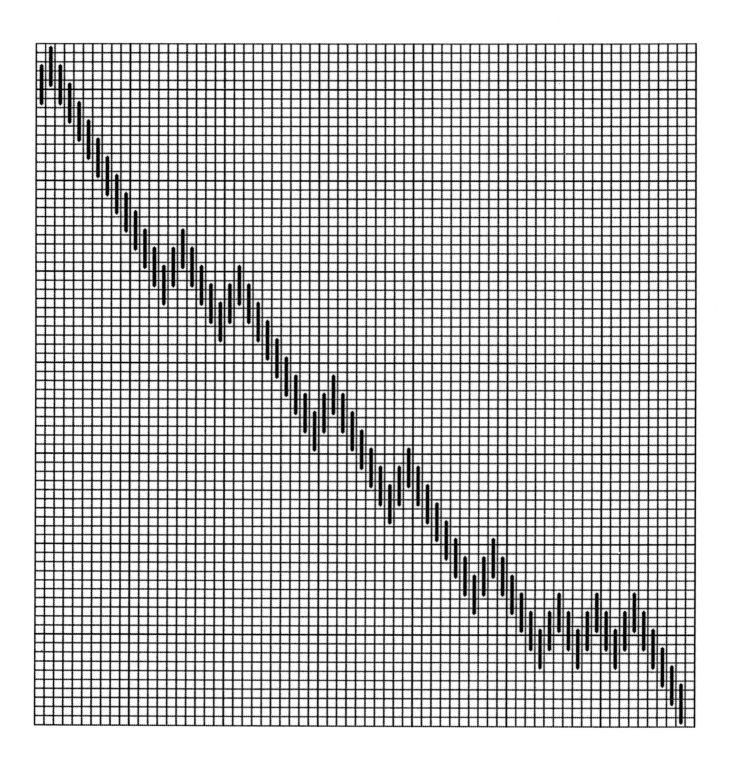

Moonlight & Gold Silk Jewel Box

9"x 9" Zweigart 18 mesh mono canvas in white
1 skein brown paper packages Silk & Ivory 01 Natural (cream)
1 skein DMC stranded Linen Ecru (cream)
1 spool Kreinik 1/16" ribbon 3232 (pale gold)
1 skein Caron Collection Watercolours 000 Natural (cream)
1 Needlepoint of Back Bay Silk Dupionni Jewel Box

This is an elegant yet simple design. It is a variation of Bargello done in a single color in different threads. Over the years I've made several pieces in a single color, but I keep coming back to all-white designs. I have made several pillows and a mini-stocking, among other items. The color picture can't really do justice to the elegant look of this color scheme.

The saturated colors of the silk box really set off the stitching. This design will work in any color of jewel box. I wanted the design to echo the elegance of the silk, so my shiny thread is a pale gold. Adding this thread to the creamy moonlight color of the matte threads, gives the piece its name.

The key to making a successful single color Bargello is finding threads with contrasting textures. Put the matte threads next to a thread which is more shiny. If you are planning on using threads like metallics, or rayons, use them sparingly, as they can change the balance of the design. They should always have the overall color as a component. For example the metallic ribbon is pale gold with lots of white in it. One effective way to use metallics would be to include them as the flames in the Flame pattern (page **) or as all the centers in a pattern like Counterchange (page **). If you do use metallics, be sure to pick one which is close in color to the other threads in your design.

Using a permanent non-Xylene or dye-based marker, mark a square 5" x 5" on your canvas.

Begin by stitching the entire outline using Silk & Ivory, starting in the center of the canvas. Just inside the outline, make the stitches which use one strand of Watercolours. The next round of stitches is made using all six strands of the DMC Linen. The center is stitched using Kreinik ribbon.

Trim the finished stitching to within two threads of the stitching. Remove the protective paper from the box and insert the stitching. Use a butter knife or chopstick to tuck the stitching under the margins of the fabric.

~ Chart and color key on following page. ~

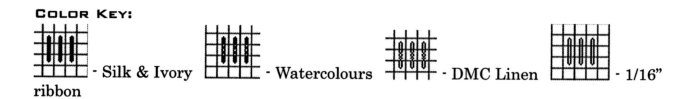

- Silk & Ivory
ribbon
- Watercolours
- DMC Linen
- 1/16"

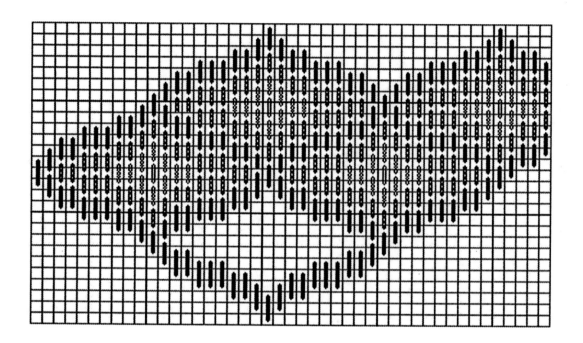

Hungarian Line Checkbook Cover

6"x8" Zweigart 18 mesh mono canvas in white
1 skein each EPiC crewel weight wool
      220 (red)
      296 (light camel)
      300 (cream)
1 Lee's Needle Arts leather checkbook cover in camel

Lee's Needle Arts makes a variety of leather goods with places for needlepoint inserts. Using these for Bargello can make a stunning accessory.

And even better, they show everyone your love of needlepoint.

This design is stitched in all wool threads. Wool wears far better than any other thread. I have another checkbook cover with wool needlepoint and it has been in my purse for years. The leather looks awful, but the needlepoint is still fresh and lovely.

The design uses two colors similar to the leather of the checkbook cover and one accent color. If you are picking your own color scheme, find a wool close to the leather color. Then pick a second shade, either lighter or darker. Finally pick an accent color. One good way to do this is to think of the leather color as a suit, and then think what kind of blouse you would wear. Buy the accent thread in that color.

The pattern is a line pattern done in Hungarianpoint. The longer stitches stick up and down alternately and are connected by diagonal lines of short stitches. This pattern is particularly effective on shapes which are wider than they are long because the repetition is quite pretty.

Trace out a rectangle 5 3/4" x 2 1/2" using a permanent non-Xylene or dye-based marker.

Begin stitching by making a line in the accent color lengthwise across the center of the area. Follow this by a line in the darker main color, a line in the lighter main color, and then a second line in the darker color. This sequence will be in between the lines of the accent color.

Because of the differing lengths of the stitches in this pattern, not every line is the same.

~ Color Key and Chart on following page. ~

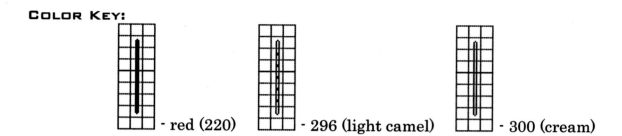

- red (220)   - 296 (light camel)   - 300 (cream)

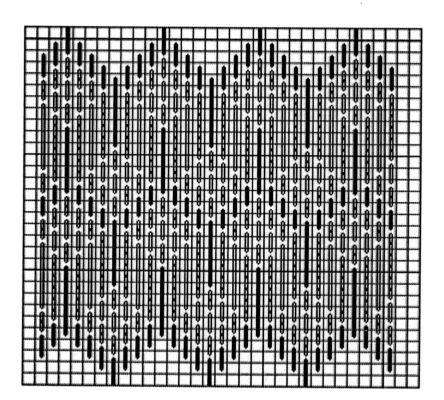

Resources

Materials for these projects are available through your local needlework shop. For shops in your area, please contact:

brown paper packages; 3730 Alexandria Pike, Cold Spring, KY 41076
Brown Sheep; (Waverly Wool) http://www.brownsheep.com
The Caron Collection; 1-800-TO-CARON http://www.caron-net.com
Conjoined Creations; http://www.conjoinedcreations.com
DMC; (satin floss, floss) http://www.dmc-usa.com, Port Kearny Bldg 10F, S. Kearny, NJ 07032
Gloriana Threads; http://www.glorianathreads.com
JL Walsh Silks; 4338 Edgewood Ave., Oakland, CA 94602
Kreinik Mfg. Inc.; 1-800-354-4255 http://www.kreinik.com
Needlepoint, Inc.; http://www.needlepointsilk.com
Rainbow Gallery; http://www.rainbowgallery.com 7412 S. Fulton Ave., #5, North Hollywood, CA 91605
River Silks; http://www.riversilks.com
Rosebud's Studio; 114 N. Francisco Street, Ste. 201, Flagstaff, AZ 86001
Sudberry House; http://www.sudberry.com, 12 Colton Rd, Old Lyme, CT 06333
The Thread Gatherer; http://www.threadgatherer.com, 2108 Norcrest, Boise, ID 83705
Ty-Di Threads; 5460-6 Sunol Blvd., Pleasanton, CA 94566
YLI, Inc.; (Shimmer Blend, Ribbon Floss) http://www.ylicorp.com
Zweigart; (canvas) (US distributor) http://www.fleurdeparis.com

Several of the designs use finishing supplies available from these sources:

Lee Needle Arts (leather goods)
Needlepoint of Back Bay (jewelry case)
Patti Paints (tote bag) http://www.pattipaints.com
Stirling (leather tool tote) http://www.stirlingcases.com
Sudberry House (coasters & box)
Yarn Tree (bellpull hardware) Ames, Iowa, 1-800-247-3952, http://www.yarntree.com

Finishing services were provided by:

Susan Thompson, The Finisher and Consultant of Arizona, contact her at susan-thompson@hotmail.com.

Bargello Books to Buy

These are some of my favorite books on Bargello. Most of these books are older and out-of-print. You can find them easily, however, at library sales, on eBay, and at used book stores. This is the way I have bought many of them.

Barnes, Charles and David P. Blake, Bargello and Related Stitchery, (Great Neck, NY; Hearthside Press), 1971.

Boyles, Margaret. Bargello: An Explosion in Color, (New York, Macmillan), 1974.

_____, The Margaret Boylles Bargello Workbook, (New York, Macmillan), 1976.

Dettelbach, Iona, Creating Contemporary Bargello, (self-published), 2007.

Fischer, Pauline and Anabel Lasker, Bargello Magic. (New York; Holt, Rinehart and Winston), 1972.

Hall, Nancy and Jean Riley, Bargello Borders, (Ann Arbor, MI; Edwards Brothers), 1974.

Kastener, Dorothy, Bargello Antics, (New York; Charles Scrbner's Sons),1979.

_____, Bargello Needlepoint, (New York; Charles Scrbner's Sons), 1974.

_____, Four Way Bargello, (New York; Charles Scrbner's Sons), 1972.

McKnight, June; The Best Bargello Book, (self-published), 2008.

Muller, Barbara, Florentine Embroidery, (Wellingborough, England; Thorsons Publishers) 1989.

Paine, Josephine Ruth, Bargello Stars, Shells and Borders, (Athens, GA; The University of Georgia, Georgia Center for Continuing Education), 1995.

Phelan, Dorothy, Traditional Bargello, (New York; St.Martin's Press), 1991.

Rome, Carol Cheney, A New Look at Bargello, (New York; Crown Publishers), 1973.

Snook, Barbara, Florentine Canvas Embroidery, (London, B.T. Batsford) ,1967.

Stevens, Gigs, Free-form Bargello, (New York; Charles Scribner's Sons), 1977.

Williams, Elsa, Bargello Florentine Canvas Work (New York, Van Norstrand Reinhold), 1967.

Contact Information for Bargello Projects

The teachers and companies listed here have Bargello projects available for stitchers at all levels. If an asterisk appears before the name, that individual is a teacher who may also have commercial designs. Please contact them for more information about their products and classes. Please note: Some projects are only available if you are a member or chapter member of the American Needlepoint Guild (http://www.needlepoint.org) or the Embroiderers Guild of American (http://www.egausa.org), Please contact them directly about these projects.

Amy's Keeping Me in Stitches
http://www.amybunger.com/
Amy Bunger often uses Bargello in her designs. Two wonderful new projects are Peaceful Trees and Joyful Ornaments. She also has lots of other inventive and wonderful Bargello projects.

Beautiful Bargello
has many lovely Bargello kits
(http://www.beautifulBargello.com/base.asp)

Caron Collection
http://www.caron-net.com
Several Bargello chart packs including some beginners projects and some free projects on the site.

*Dakota Rogers
http://www.dakotarogers.com/
Many of her classes and projects incorporate Bargello. Currently two of her on-line Cyberclasses, the two Potpourri classes, are of Indian Pots and feature lots of Bargello in a unique presentation. In her products, several of the composer cats use lots of Bargello.

Harbour Light Designs
Distributed by Norden Crafts
(http://www.nordencrafts.com/CHARTS/HLD/hldmain.html)

Heartfelt Designs
http://www.heartfelt-designs.com/
Tara's Purse is a lovely Bargello piece featuring overdyed threads.

Needlepoint Now
http://www.needlepointnow.com/
This popular needlepoint magazine often has Bargello projects. Many back issues with Bargello are available as well. A contemporary multi-part Bargello sampler ran beginning in the May.June 2002 issue. It's glorious.

Northern Pine Designs
http://www.northernpinedesigns.com
Bargello and Diagonal Bargello projects listed in the "needlepoint" category in several subcategories.

*Pat Mazu
Distributed by Stitches from the Heart (http://www.stitches-heart.com/patmazu/)
She is particularly well-known for her mini-socks, many of which feature Bargello. Several of these are in older issues of ANG's Chapter Project Book. The current (2007) Chapter Project Book (http://www.needlepoint.org/CPB/2007.php) has a marvelous Four-way Bargello pattern, which I'm about to start.

Rainbow Gallery
http://www.rainbowgallery.com
Several books and charts by Iona Dettelbach, including a series which increases in difficulty. Shops can access their free designs for 2008 which feature Bargello. Some needlepoint free charts feature Bargello as well.

Jim Wurth
jwurth@msn.com
Has an intricate Bargello design, Bargello 2025.

About the Author

Janet Perry is one of the leading writers of needlepoint stitch guides in America with guides currently available for canvases for over 20 designers. Bargello has been one of her needlepoint passions since she first learned to stitch it in 1971 (at 14). She loves the simplicity of the stitch combined with the endless possibilities for color and pattern. This book represents 20 years of learning, stitching, and teaching Bargello.

Janet specializes in making needlepoint, a new old-fashioned craft, fun, easy and affordable. She's well-known for her ability to make seemingly difficult techniques easy and for making easy techniques, like Bargello, fresh and creative.

She is the author of the popular blog and newsletter, Nuts about Needlepoint (http://www.nuts-about-needlepoint.com) and has written for many leading consumer and trade publications on needlework.

She lives in the Napa Valley with her family and cats and is working on her third book, a collection of stories about needlework which will be published in late 2008.

Visit the Bargello Revisited website at
http://www.napaneedlepoint.com/bargellohome.html